30-minute entertaining

30-minute entertaining

Louise Pickford

Photography by Ian Wallace

hamlyn

A Pyramid Paperback from Hamlyn

First published in Great Britain in 1998 by Hamlyn,
a division of Octopus Publishing Group Ltd
2–4 Heron Quays, London E14 4JP

This revised edition published 2004

Copyright © Octopus Publishing Group Ltd 2004

ISBN 0 600 61028 4

A CIP catalogue record for this book is available
from the British Library

Printed and bound in China

10 9 8 7 6 5 4 3 2 1

NOTES

1 The Department of Health advises that eggs
should not be consumed raw. It is prudent for
more vulnerable people such as pregnant and
nursing mothers, invalids, the elderly, babies and
young children to avoid uncooked or lightly cooked
dishes made with eggs.

2 Meat and poultry should be cooked thoroughly.
To test if poultry is cooked, pierce the flesh
through the thickest part with a skewer or fork –
the juices should run clear, never pink or red.

3 This book includes dishes made with nuts and
nut derivatives. It is advisable for those with
known allergic reactions to nuts and nut
derivatives and those who may be potentially
vulnerable to these allergies, such as pregnant and
nursing mothers, invalids, the elderly, babies and
children, to avoid dishes made with nuts and nut
oils. It is also prudent to check the labels of pre-
prepared ingredients for the possible inclusion of
nut derivatives.

contents

introduction

With increased awareness of the different cultures around the world, the result of exposure to travel and the media, new and exciting products and foods with an exotic nature have become almost commonplace. Supermarkets now stock ingredients that until recently were enjoyed only in their countries of origin.

Many of these foods travel well and can be used to great effect, particularly staples, canned and bottled items. However, some imported fresh ingredients have been picked under-ripe and never produce the flavour they would have had if left to ripen on the plant.

I think I probably fell in love with food years before I became aware just how much I really do love it. Growing up on a farm where good-quality meat, dairy products, vegetables and fruit were taken for granted, I assumed all food tasted that way. Boarding school food soon changed all that, but as a typical teenager there were other priorities and the enjoyment of food came down to what was in the tuck shop.

I can't pretend to have shown much interest in cooking at home. My mother was and still is a great cook, but with no disrespect, her food was unadventurous. It was simply great traditional British cooking. I suspect I did very little to help, but I must have inherited my mother's love of food because I have become an enthusiastic and passionate cook.

Today I make my living by cooking and writing recipes and I feel just as passionate now as I did when I began. What has changed are the sources of my inspirations, through travel, the availability of fresh produce, and people's lifestyles and attitudes towards cooking. All of these factors have gone towards defining the recipes in this book.

I cook professionally every day, so when I do cook for pleasure for myself, family or friends I don't want to spend hours preparing ingredients. Similarly, with most people's lifestyles, leisure time is at a premium. Quick, simple and delicious food is of the highest importance, and I hope that the dishes in this book satisfy those criteria. I have thought hard about the way we eat and the occasions when we may be entertaining, so that you should be able to find a recipe for every event, time of year and time of day. For instance, this book begins with the first meal of the day – breakfast – but also includes brunch dishes and recipes for mid-morning snacks. The collection of party foods is very useful as it proves that canapés don't have to be excruciatingly fiddly and time-consuming to impress. Dinner parties for two or more won't need to take hours to put together or cause any stress, as you'll find plenty of recipes in the Two's Company and Posh Nosh chapters that can be prepared with ease.

Practicalities All the recipes in the book have been developed so that they can be prepared and cooked within 30 minutes. It has been quite a challenge to achieve this, as you do not want to compromise the flavour of the dish just to make it quickly. (There are other occasions when you can potter and time is of no consequence.) So I have selected dishes that meet both criteria – to taste great but take no more than 30 minutes.

Of course there are many dishes that are ready in a flash, especially those with little or no cooking involved. You will find that about 40 of the recipes can be ready in under 20 minutes, which really is 'fast' food.

The 30 minutes stated includes all the preparation on the assumption that the oven has been preheated, water for cooking pasta is already boiling, and so on. This is so that I can offer a wide range of recipes and it seems mad to omit a recipe because you have to wait an extra 10 minutes for the oven to come to the required temperature. The recipes are easy to follow and very organized – you can be chopping vegetables while the pasta is cooking, for example. Read the recipes through before you start, get pots and pans ready, heat the serving plates and dishes and the rest is a breeze.

Nearly all the ingredients in the book are widely available and the glossary will clarify queries on any of the unusual products and where they can be found. It is important in all cooking to buy the freshest produce available, so always shop at a reliable store that you know well, especially for fresh fish and meat. Vegetables and fruit can be found in supermarkets, but a good-quality greengrocer will offer even fresher ingredients and it's always worth a trip to ethnic food stores, not only for the freshest of ingredients, but simply to view the range of unusual and fascinating foods – most large cities will have at least one Oriental or Asian food store.

Herbs used are always fresh, unless otherwise stated; you can keep fresh herbs wrapped in a plastic bag in the refrigerator for 3–4 days. I recommend sea salt and always crush peppercorns just before using to get the maximum flavour. Olive oil, for use on salads, should be extra virgin, preferably from a single estate, which will be indicated on the bottle. Meat should be free-range where possible, not just for the ethics, but because it really will have more flavour than intensively reared meats.

Sharing food with friends should be a relaxing and sociable pastime. It doesn't have to be a formal event or a meal on a grand scale – a simple supper or lunch with a glass or two of wine, al fresco in the summer, is time out from an otherwise hectic day. All this in under 30 minutes – a culinary nirvana!

glossary

Black sesame seeds These are the same as the pale golden sesame seeds used extensively in Middle Eastern and Asian cooking. Use in the same way, roasting before use to add a delicious nutty flavour to foods.

Buttermilk Originally the liquid extracted from cream during butter-making. Today 'cultured buttermilk' is made with skimmed milk and treated with a fermentation culture then heat-treated to kill bacteria. It has a slight sourness.

Crab meat White crab meat is available fresh in vacuum packs from good fishmongers, or you can buy mixed crab meat either frozen or prepared in the shell.

Fish sauce Essential in the cooking of South-east Asia, fish sauce is made by fermenting small fish in brine. The liquid that is drawn off is then matured in the sun before being bottled. Use in a similar way to soy sauce for adding flavour to foods. It is called *nam pla* in Thailand and *nuoc mam* in Vietnam.

Five-spice seasoning This is a mixture of ground spices used in Chinese cooking. It is a combination of star anise, cloves, fennel, cassia (Chinese cinnamon) and Szechuan pepper. Add sparingly to savoury dishes as the flavour is intense.

Framboise A raspberry liqueur.

Horseradish Fresh horseradish, in season during spring in Britain, is rarely available in our stores. Use grated horseradish, available in jars from larger supermarkets and Jewish food stores.

Jerk seasoning A ready-made spice mix used in West Indian and Creole cooking. It is made up from allspice, cinnamon, nutmeg, thyme, sugar and chilli.

Jerusalem artichokes These tubers, originating from North America, are not related to globe artichokes. They are knobbly greyish brown tubers, roughly oval in shape. They have a sweet, nutty flavour and can be roasted or boiled and mashed.

Kecap manis This is the name given to sweet soy sauce in Indonesia. It is available from most supermarkets and Asian stores.

Lemon grass This is a grass indigenous to tropical Asia, with a pungent lemon flavour that is released when the stalk is crushed or cut. It is used extensively in Asian cooking to flavour soups and stews and is now widely available in supermarkets.

Lime leaves These come from a lime which is generally known as the 'kaffir' lime although its true name is the makrut lime. The leaves release an intense aromatic lime flavour when they are torn or bruised. Lime leaves are used extensively in Thai, Vietnamese and Malay cooking.

Marinated artichokes Small artichokes that have been cooked, charred and then stored in oil. Available from Italian delicatessens and specialist food stores.

Mirin Not rice wine, as it is often mistakenly called, but a spirit-based drink used in Japanese cooking. It has a high alcohol content and is added to marinades, sauces and soups. You can use sake instead, but remember that mirin is sweeter, so add a little sugar.

Miso A Japanese fermented 'bean paste' available from Japanese stores and health food shops. It is available as rice, barley or rye miso and you can use any one as preferred.

Mussels Farmed mussels are becoming more readily available and tend to be far cleaner than those that live and grow in the 'wild'. Consequently, they are easier to clean.

Nori These are the flat sheets of seaweed used to make sushi. Available from some supermarkets and health food stores.

Palm sugar This unprocessed sugar comes from various palms or from sugar cane and is used as a sweetener in South-east Asia. It is sold in cylindrical shapes, rounded cakes or in jars and varies in colour from pale gold to dark brown. It is sometimes called jaggery.

Pea shoots The shoots from young peas, these are generally available only to those who are lucky enough to grow their own. However, some herb and salad suppliers are beginning to sell pea shoots, so keep an eye open as supermarkets are bound to follow.

Pomegranate syrup This thick, dark syrup, extracted from sour pomegranates, is widely used in North African and Middle Eastern cooking. It has a sharp-sweet flavour. Available from specialist food stores, there is no real equivalent.

Quince paste Made from quinces, which belong to the apple family, quince paste or preserve is sometimes sold as membrillo paste (the Spanish name) and can be found in some supermarkets or specialist food stores.

Rice flour pancakes Sold dried, these are very thin round rice flour pancakes that need to be rehydrated before use. Follow the packet instructions.

Rice noodles Noodles made from rice flour, used in Asian cooking. There are two main types that are sold dried: rice vermicelli noodles, which are thin threads, and the larger flat rice noodles, which are similar to tagliatelle.

Rosewater First used by the ancient Greeks, Egyptians and Romans, this fragrant water is extracted from roses and added to sweet and savoury dishes. Available from Middle Eastern stores and some supermarkets.

Sake A strong alcoholic Japanese drink often referred to as rice wine, sake is used extensively in Japanese cooking. Mirin can be used instead.

Soba noodles These are Japanese buckwheat noodles, sold dried, and widely available from health food stores.

Thai seven-spice seasoning A ready mix of Thai spices.

Smoke mix Smoking foods over a mixture of tea leaves, sugar and rice is common in Chinese cooking and adds an intensely smoky flavour to fish and meat. For the recipes in this book, mix 8 tablespoons each of Jasmine tea leaves, soft brown sugar and long-grain rice.

Tamarind pulp Extracted from the pod of the tamarind tree, a native of Africa, India and the Far East. The seeds are surrounded by a thick gooey pulp which has a pleasantly sour taste. It is used to flavour soups, stews and pastes in South-east Asian dishes. Available ready-pulped from some supermarkets and Oriental food shops.

morning foods

Many of us have such hectic lifestyles that breakfast has become nothing more than a quick cuppa and, perhaps, toast or a bowl of cereal. We all know that eating a good breakfast is vital in kick-starting both body and mind into action. The following recipes are designed to do just that, so whether it's a weekday breakfast, weekend brunch or just a mid-morning snack, take a few extra moments and treat yourself.

poached eggs with parma ham and herb tomatoes

preparation time **5 mins**
cooking time **10–12 mins**
total time **15–17 mins** serves **4**

4 ripe tomatoes
2 tablespoons chopped basil
4 tablespoons extra virgin olive oil
4 slices Parma ham
4 large eggs
salt and pepper
hot buttered muffins, to serve

one Halve the tomatoes and place them, cut-side up, on a grill pan. Mix the basil with 2 tablespoons of the oil and drizzle over the cut tomatoes. Season well with salt and pepper. Cook under a preheated grill for about 6–7 minutes, until softened. Remove and keep warm.
two Meanwhile, heat the remaining olive oil in a frying pan and fry the Parma ham until crisp. Drain on kitchen paper and keep warm while you cook the eggs.
three Poach the eggs in gently simmering water or an egg poacher for 3–4 minutes. Serve on buttered toasted muffins with the ham and grilled tomatoes.

This is a healthier version of a traditional 'fry-up'.

boiled egg with anchovy soldiers

preparation time **5 mins**
cooking time **5 mins**
total time **10 mins** serves **4**

8 anchovy fillets in oil, drained
50 g/2 oz unsalted butter, softened
4 large eggs
4 thick slices white bread
pepper
mustard and cress, to serve

one Wash the anchovies, pat dry with kitchen paper and then chop them finely. Beat them into the softened butter and season with pepper.
two Boil the eggs for 4–5 minutes, until softly set. Meanwhile, toast the bread, butter one side with the anchovy butter and cut into fingers.
three Serve the eggs with the anchovy toasts and some mustard and cress.

Boiled eggs with fingers of toast, or 'soldiers', is a
reminder of childhood. Who wants to grow up, anyway?

tropical fruits with spiced syrup

preparation time **10 mins**, plus cooling
cooking time **2 mins**
total time **20 mins** serves **4**

1 lime
1 piece of stem ginger, diced
2 tablespoons syrup from the ginger jar
2 star anise
4 tablespoons water
½ large cantaloupe melon
1 large mango
1 large papaya
½ pomegranate, to decorate (optional)
fromage frais, to serve

one Peel the lime and cut the rind into thin strips. Squeeze the lime juice into a small pan. Add the stem ginger to the pan with the lime rind, ginger syrup, star anise and water. Simmer for 2 minutes and immediately plunge the base of the pan into some iced water to cool the syrup.
two Meanwhile, prepare the fruit. Cut the melon into quarters, remove the seeds and cut the flesh into wedges. Peel the mango, remove the stone and cut the flesh into quarters. Peel and deseed the papaya and quarter the flesh.
three Arrange the fruits on plates, spoon over the spiced syrup, decorate with a few pomegranate seeds, if using, and serve with fromage frais.

The perfect breakfast for
a summer's morning.

buttermilk pancakes with blueberry sauce

preparation time **10 mins**
cooking time **3–4 mins** per batch,
  16 mins for **12**
total time **26 mins** serves **4–6**

250 g/8 oz fresh blueberries
2 tablespoons clear honey
dash of lemon juice
15 g/½ oz butter
150 g/5 oz self-raising flour
1 teaspoon bicarbonate of soda
40 g/1½ oz caster sugar
1 egg, beaten
350 ml/12 fl oz buttermilk
Greek yogurt or crème fraîche, to serve
icing sugar, for dusting

one Warm the berries with the honey and a dash of lemon juice in a small saucepan for about 3 minutes, until they release their juices. Keep warm.
two Melt the butter in a small pan. Sift together the flour and bicarbonate of soda in a bowl and stir in the sugar. Beat together the egg and buttermilk and gradually whisk the mixture into the dry ingredients with the melted butter to make a smooth batter.
three Heat a nonstick frying pan until hot and drop in large spoonfuls of batter. Cook for 3 minutes, until bubbles appear on the surface. Flip the pancakes over and cook for a further minute. Keep them warm in a low oven while cooking the rest.
four Serve the pancakes topped with the blueberry sauce and some Greek yogurt or crème fraîche. Dust with a little icing sugar to decorate.

celeriac rösti with smoked eel and horseradish

preparation time **10 mins**
cooking time **15 mins**
total time **25 mins** serves **4**

250 g/8 oz celeriac, finely grated
250 g/8 oz waxy potatoes, finely grated
4 thyme sprigs
2 tablespoons extra virgin olive oil
175 g/6 oz smoked eel fillets
2 teaspoons grated horseradish
4 tablespoons crème fraîche
salt and pepper
lemon wedges, to garnish
peppery salad leaves, to serve
    (optional)

one Combine the celeriac and potatoes in a bowl. Strip the thyme stalks of their leaves, add the leaves to the vegetables and season with plenty of salt and pepper. Shape into four large cakes about 10 cm/ 4 inches in diameter and 2.5 cm/1 inch deep.
two Heat the oil in a large nonstick frying pan, add the cakes and fry for 5 minutes on each side, until browned and reduced in height. Drain on kitchen paper.
three Meanwhile, carefully flake the eel and toss with the horseradish and crème fraîche. Season with salt and pepper.
four Top each rösti with some of the smoked eel mixture and serve with lemon wedges and some salad leaves, if liked.

Add some peppery salad leaves dressed with olive oil and lemon juice if you are serving this as a brunch dish.

herb omelette with mustard mushrooms

preparation time **5 mins**
cooking time **10 mins**
total time **15 mins** serves **2**

1 tablespoon wholegrain mustard
50 g/2 oz butter, softened
4 flat mushrooms
2 tablespoons chopped mixed herbs (such
   as chives, parsley and tarragon)
4 eggs
salt and pepper

one Beat the mustard into 40 g/1½ oz of the butter and spread over the undersides of the mushrooms. Place them on a foil-lined grill pan and cook for 5–6 minutes until golden and tender. Remove and keep warm.
two Meanwhile, beat the herbs into the eggs and season with salt and pepper.
three Melt the remaining butter in an omelette or nonstick frying pan, swirl in the egg mixture and cook until almost set. Carefully slide the omelette and flip it over on to a warmed plate, add the mushrooms and serve immediately.

If you prefer, cook half the egg mixture at a time to make two smaller omelettes.

honeyed ricotta with summer fruits

preparation time **10 mins**
total time **10 mins** serves **4**

125 g/4 oz raspberries
2 teaspoons rosewater
2 tablespoons pumpkin seeds
250 g/8 oz ricotta cheese
250 g/8 oz mixed summer berries
2 tablespoons clear honey with honeycomb
a pinch of ground cinnamon

one Rub the raspberries through a fine sieve to purée, then mix them with the rosewater. Alternatively, process together in a food processor or blender and then sieve to remove the pips. Toast the pumpkin seeds.
two Slice the ricotta into wedges and arrange on plates with the berries. Drizzle the honey and raspberry purée over the ricotta, adding a little honeycomb, and serve scattered with the pumpkin seeds and a sprinkling of cinnamon.

lemon and cinnamon crêpes

preparation time **5 mins**
cooking time **1½ mins per batch**,
 24 mins for all 16
total time **29 mins** serves **5–8**

15 g/½ oz butter
125 g/4 oz plain flour
½ teaspoon ground cinnamon
a pinch of salt
1 teaspoon grated lemon rind
1 egg, beaten
300 ml/½ pint milk
vegetable oil, for frying

TO SERVE
sugar
lemon wedges

one Melt the butter in a small pan. Sift the flour, cinnamon, salt and grated lemon rind into a bowl, make a well in the centre and gradually beat in the egg, milk and melted butter to make a smooth batter.
two Lightly brush a crêpe pan or small frying pan with vegetable oil. Heat until smoking, then pour in a small ladleful of batter, swirling it to the edges of the pan.
three Cook the crêpe for 1 minute until lightly golden underneath, then gently flip it over and cook for a further 30 seconds. Keep it warm while cooking the remainder.
four Serve 2–3 crêpes per person, dusted with sugar and with some lemon wedges.

triple chocolate muffins

preparation time **12 mins**
cooking time **12 mins**
total time **24 mins** serves **6**

50 g/2 oz plain chocolate chips
50 g/2 oz unsalted butter
2 eggs
75 g/3 oz caster sugar
75 g/3 oz self-raising flour
25 g/1 oz cocoa powder
25 g/1 oz white chocolate chips

one Melt the plain chocolate chips with the butter in a small pan over a low heat. Beat together the eggs, sugar, flour and cocoa powder in a large bowl. With a metal spatula, fold in the melted chocolate mixture and the white chocolate chips.
two Spoon the mixture into a bun tray lined with paper cases and bake in a preheated oven, 180°C (350°F), Gas Mark 4, for 12 minutes, until risen and firm to the touch.
three Transfer the muffins to a wire rack to cool slightly before eating.

spiced chocolate pastries

preparation time **15 mins**
cooking time **12 mins**
total time **27 mins** makes **9**

250 g/8 oz puff pastry, thawed if frozen
flour, for dusting
1 egg yolk
2 tablespoons milk
18 squares dark chocolate
1 teaspoon grated orange rind
a pinch of ground star anise
butter, for greasing

one Roll out the pastry thinly on a clean, lightly floured surface and trim to form a 23 cm/9 inch square. Cut the pastry into three crossways and lengthways so that you have 9 squares.
two Beat the egg yolk with the milk to make a glaze and brush a little around the edges of the squares.
three Place 2 squares of chocolate, a little orange rind and a touch of star anise on each one. Fold diagonally in half and press the edges together to seal.
four Place the pastries on a greased baking sheet and bake in a preheated oven, 200°C (400°F), Gas Mark 6, for 12 minutes, until risen and golden. Leave to cool on a wire rack for a few minutes before serving.

Delicious with a mug of tea
or freshly brewed coffee.

Hazelnut cookies that literally 'melt' in the mouth.

melon and ginger cooler

preparation time **10 mins**
total time **10 mins** serves **2**

1 large ripe galia melon, halved
   and deseeded
4 mint sprigs
2.5 cm/1 inch piece of fresh root ginger,
   peeled and grated
1 tablespoon lime cordial
1 tablespoon lime juice
a handful of crushed ice

one Scoop the melon flesh into a food processor or blender. Strip the mint leaves from the stalks. Add the mint leaves, ginger, lime cordial and lime juice to the melon and process until smooth.
two Half-fill two tall glasses with crushed ice and top up with the melon purée. Serve immediately.

quick hazelnut melts

preparation time **10 mins**
cooking time **12 mins**
total time **22 mins** makes **20**

50 g/2 oz blanched hazelnuts
125 g/4 oz butter, softened, plus extra
   for greasing
50 g/2 oz caster sugar
150 g/5 oz plain flour

one Grind the hazelnuts in a food processor until fairly smooth, but still retaining a little texture. Dry-fry in a heavy-based frying pan over a low heat until evenly golden. Tip into a bowl and stir until cool.
two Blend together the butter and sugar in the food processor until creamy. Add the flour and cooled nuts and process again to make a soft dough.
three Take walnut-size pieces of dough and shape into rolls, then pat them into flat ovals. Place the biscuits on a greased baking sheet and bake in a preheated oven, 190°C (375°F), Gas Mark 5, for 12 minutes, until just golden. Cool on a wire rack.

mango and coconut lassi

preparation time **10 mins**
total time **10 mins** serves **2–4**

1 large ripe mango
juice of 1 orange
juice of 1 lime
1 tablespoon clear honey
300 ml/½ pint natural yogurt
4 tablespoons coconut milk
ice cubes, to serve

one Peel the mango, cut out the stone
and finely dice the flesh (you will need
about 250 g/8 oz). Place the flesh in a food
processor or blender.
two Add the orange juice, lime juice, honey,
yogurt and coconut milk and process until
smooth. Chill or serve immediately with
some ice cubes.

cardamom coffee affogato

preparation time **10 mins**
total time **10 mins** serves **4**

4 tablespoons fresh espresso coffee beans
seeds from 2 cardamom pods
4–8 scoops vanilla ice cream
crystal sugar sticks, to serve (optional)

one Grind the beans and cardamom seeds
in a spice grinder until they are sufficiently
ground for your coffee maker.
two Make a pot of strong coffee in the
normal way using the newly ground
cardamom coffee and pour into coffee
cups or heat-proof glasses.
three Add the scoops of ice cream to the
coffee and serve immediately with crystal
sugar sticks, if using.

This spiced coffee takes its
name from the Italian word
for drowning – the scoops of
ice cream slowly 'drown' in
the coffee making this a real
mid-morning treat. It can also
be served as an after-dinner
coffee or with chocolate ice
cream for a mocha flavour.

light lunches

Over the past 30 years or so, the way we work has determined the way we eat and today the main meal is in the evening. A leisurely lunch is a bit of a treat, especially mid-week, so why not indulge yourself and friends with one of the following dishes? Light and quick to prepare, you can satisfy your hunger without overdoing it!

noodle soup with prawn tempura

preparation time **20 mins**
cooking time **10 mins**
total time **30 mins** serves **4**

125 g/4 oz soba noodles
12 raw tiger prawns
1 bunch spring onions, trimmed
2 pak choi
2 sheets nori
2 teaspoons sesame oil
1.8 litres/3 pints hot vegetable stock
4 tablespoons sake
2 tablespoons dark soy sauce
125 g/4 oz bean sprouts
vegetable oil, for deep-frying

TEMPURA
1 egg yolk
50 g/2 oz plain flour
100 ml/3½ fl oz iced water

one Cook the noodles according to packet instructions. Meanwhile, peel and devein the prawns (see page 33). Heat the vegetable oil to 180–190°C (350–375°F), until a cube of bread browns in 30 seconds.

two To make the soup, slice the spring onions and shred the pak choi and nori. Heat the sesame oil in a large wok and stir-fry the onions and pak choi for 1 minute. Add the stock, sake, soy sauce and sugar and simmer gently for 5 minutes. Then stir in the bean sprouts.

three Meanwhile, make the tempura batter. Briefly whisk together the egg yolk, flour and water to make a slightly lumpy batter. Dip the prawns into the batter and deep-fry in the hot oil for 3 minutes, until golden. Drain on kitchen paper.

four Divide the noodles between serving bowls, add the soup and top with the prawns and strips of nori.

chilled gazpacho with indian flavours

preparation time **15 mins**
freezing time **15 mins**
total time **30 mins** serves **4**

1 small red onion, chopped
2 garlic cloves, chopped
2.5 cm/1 inch piece of fresh root ginger,
   peeled and grated
1 small red pepper, deseeded and chopped
2 fresh red chillies, deseeded and chopped
500 g/1 lb ripe tomatoes, chopped
2 tablespoons chopped coriander
4 poppadums, crumbled
300 ml/½ pint cold vegetable stock
300 ml/½ pint tomato juice
4 tablespoons extra virgin olive oil
2 tablespoons white wine vinegar
salt and pepper

TO GARNISH
natural yogurt
poppadums
coriander sprigs

one Place the onion, garlic, ginger, red pepper, chillies, tomatoes, coriander and poppadums in a food processor or blender and process until smooth.
two Transfer the mixture to a bowl and stir in all the remaining ingredients. Season to taste with salt and pepper. Freeze for at least 10 minutes until chilled.
three Spoon into bowls and garnish with yogurt, poppadums and coriander sprigs.

goats' cheese soufflés

preparation time **15 mins**
cooking time **12 mins**
total time **27 mins** serves **4**

25 g/1 oz unsalted butter
15 g/½ oz Parmesan cheese, grated
1 tablespoon plain flour
5 tablespoons milk
1 tablespoon chopped tarragon
1 egg yolk
100 g/3½ oz goats' cheese, diced
3 egg whites
salt and pepper

one Melt half the butter. Brush the insides of 4 ramekin dishes with the melted butter and dust with the Parmesan. Place the ramekins on a baking sheet.
two Melt the remaining butter and stir in the flour. Cook over a low heat, stirring constantly, for 30 seconds. Remove from the heat and gradually stir in the milk. Return to the heat and stir until the mixture boils and thickens. Transfer to a bowl.
three Beat the tarragon into the sauce with the egg yolk and goats' cheese. Season lightly with salt and pepper. Whisk the egg whites and fold them in.
four Spoon into the ramekins and bake in a preheated oven, 200°C (400°F), Gas Mark 6, for 12 minutes, until the soufflés are risen and golden. Serve immediately.

spinach, artichoke and bacon salad with a warm dressing

preparation time **8 mins**
cooking time **20 mins**
total time **28 mins** serves **4**

4 small Jerusalem artichokes
2 tablespoons walnut oil
8 slices smoked pancetta
40 g/1½ oz walnuts
4–6 tablespoons extra virgin olive oil
1 garlic clove, crushed
2 tablespoons balsamic vinegar
125 g/4 oz baby spinach leaves
50 g/2 oz watercress
4 tablespoons chopped mixed herbs (such
    as basil, mint and parsley)
salt and pepper

one Scrub the artichokes and cut them into
5 mm/¼ inch thick slices. Toss with the
walnut oil in a roasting tin and roast in a
preheated oven, 200°C (400°F), Gas Mark 6,
for 20 minutes, turning after 10 minutes.
two Meanwhile, grill the pancetta until
crisp, then break it into bite-sized pieces.
Dry-fry the walnuts until evenly browned.
Set aside.
three Heat 1 tablespoon of the olive oil in
a small pan and fry the garlic for 1 minute,
until lightly golden. Add the vinegar and the
remaining olive oil, season to taste with salt
and pepper and keep warm.
four Put the spinach and watercress in a
large bowl, add the pancetta, walnuts,
artichokes and herbs and mix well. Drizzle
with the warm dressing. Serve immediately.

charred leek salad with hazelnuts

preparation time **10 mins**
cooking time **14 mins**
total time **24 mins** serves **4**

500 g/1 lb baby leeks
1–2 tablespoons hazelnut oil
dash of lemon juice
40 g/1½ oz blanched hazelnuts
2 little gem or Cos lettuce hearts
a few mint sprigs
15 g/½ oz Pecorino cheese
20 black olives, to garnish

DRESSING
4 tablespoons hazelnut oil
2 tablespoons extra virgin olive oil
2 teaspoons sherry vinegar
salt and pepper

one Brush the leeks with a little hazelnut oil
and griddle or grill, turning frequently, for
6–8 minutes, until evenly browned and
cooked through. Toss with a dash of lemon
juice and season to taste with salt and
pepper. Set aside to cool.
two Meanwhile, dry-fry the hazelnuts until
browned, cool slightly and then roughly
chop. Separate the lettuce leaves and pull
the mint leaves from their stalks.
three Arrange the leeks in bowls or on
plates and top with the lettuce leaves, mint
and nuts. Whisk the dressing ingredients
together and pour over the salad. Shave the
pecorino over the salad and serve garnished
with the olives.

To devein prawns, cut down the length of the middle of the curved
back of the peeled prawn with a sharp knife. Remove the intestinal vein
with the tip of the knife or your fingers.

sesame steamed prawns

preparation time **15 mins**
cooking time **5 mins**
total time **20 mins** serves **4**

16 raw tiger prawns, peeled, with tails
    intact and deveined
2 garlic cloves, sliced
1 red chilli, deseeded and chopped
grated rind and juice of 1 lime
2.5 cm/1 inch piece root ginger, peeled
    and chopped
2 tablespoons rice wine
2 tablespoons Thai fish sauce
4 Savoy cabbage leaves
1 tablespoon sesame oil
salt
a few coriander, mint and basil leaves,
    to garnish

one First butterfly the prawns. Cut down the deveined slit on the back of the prawns so they will open up and lie flat, leaving the tail intact. Wash and pat dry.

two Mix the garlic, chilli, lime rind and juice, ginger, rice wine and fish sauce in a bowl. Add the prawns and toss well. Set aside.

three Blanch the cabbage leaves in lightly salted boiling water for 30 seconds, then drain and refresh under cold water. Pat dry.

four Arrange the cabbage leaves in a bamboo steamer and carefully spoon the prawns and their marinade on top of the leaves. Cover and steam for 2–3 minutes, until the prawns are pink.

five Meanwhile, heat the sesame oil. Place the cabbage leaves and prawns on a serving dish. Pour the hot oil over them and scatter with the herbs.

skate with sage butter

preparation time **5 mins**
cooking time **22 mins**
total time **27 mins** serves **4**

1 large skate wing
125 g/4 oz unsalted butter
2 tablespoons chopped sage
4 tablespoons capers in brine, drained
    and rinsed
2 tablespoons balsamic vinegar
125 ml/4 fl oz hot fish or vegetable stock
a dash of lemon juice
salt and pepper

one Wash and dry the skate wing and cut it as evenly as possible into 4 portions. Season lightly with salt and pepper. Melt 25 g/1 oz of the butter in a large frying pan and fry the skate for 4–5 minutes each side, until just browned. Remove from the heat and keep warm.

two Wipe out the frying pan and melt the remaining butter. When it stops foaming, add the sage leaves and fry until golden. Stir in the capers, vinegar and stock and simmer until reduced slightly.

three Season to taste with salt, pepper and lemon juice. Drizzle the sage butter over the skate and serve immediately.

swordfish ciabatta with salsa rossa

preparation time **10 mins**
cooking time **20 mins**
total time **30 mins** serves **4**

1 large red pepper, quartered and deseeded
2 tablespoons extra virgin olive oil,
    plus extra for brushing
1 garlic clove, crushed
2 ripe tomatoes, peeled and chopped
a pinch of dried chilli flakes
1 teaspoon dried oregano
1 large ciabatta
4 thinly cut swordfish steaks,
    about 100 g/3½ oz each
salt and pepper
salad leaves, to serve
lemon wedges, to garnish

This is a steak sandwich with a healthy difference. Ask your fishmonger to cut the swordfish into 5 mm/¼ inch slices.

one Place the red pepper under a preheated grill and cook for 3–4 minutes each side, until charred and tender. Transfer to a plastic bag and set aside to cool for 5 minutes.
two Meanwhile, heat half the oil in a small pan and fry the garlic for 30 seconds. Add the tomatoes, chilli flakes and oregano and simmer for 5 minutes.
three Using rubber gloves to protect your hands if the pepper is still hot, peel the skin and dice the flesh. Add to the tomato mixture and cook for a further 5 minutes, until the sauce is thickened. Season to taste with salt and pepper and set aside.
four While the sauce is cooking, cut the ciabatta into quarters and toast on both sides. Drizzle with oil.
five Season the swordfish steaks with salt and pepper and brush with a little oil. Sear on a very hot griddle for about 30 seconds on each side and serve on the toasted bread with a spoonful of the sauce and some salad leaves. Serve garnished with lemon wedges.

warm tea smoked salmon salad with wilted rocket

preparation time **15 mins**
cooking time **5 mins**, plus resting
total time **23 mins** serves **4**

1 quantity Smoke Mix (see page 9)
4 salmon fillets, about 125 g/4 oz each
125 g/4 oz cherry tomatoes, halved
125 g/4 oz wild rocket leaves

DRESSING
1 shallot, finely chopped
1 garlic clove, finely chopped
a few thyme sprigs
1 teaspoon Dijon mustard
2 teaspoons white wine vinegar
4–5 tablespoons extra virgin olive oil
salt and pepper

Although smoking fish and meat over a mixture of tea leaves, sugar and rice is a method widely used in Chinese cooking, in this dish the method is adapted for European tastes. You will need a wok with a lid and a trivet for this recipe.

one Line a wok with a large sheet of foil, allowing it to overhang the edges, and tip in the smoke mix. Place a trivet over the top. Cover with a tight-fitting lid and heat for 5 minutes, until the mixture is smoking.
two Meanwhile, remove any remaining bones from the salmon with a pair of tweezers. Place the tomatoes in a bowl with the rocket leaves.
three Quickly remove the lid from the wok and place the salmon fillets, skin-side down, on the trivet. Cover and cook over a high heat for 5 minutes. Remove from the heat and set aside, covered, for 3 minutes.
four Meanwhile, make the dressing. Put the shallot, garlic, thyme, mustard, vinegar and oil in a bowl and season to taste with salt and pepper. Whisk well to combine.
five Flake the salmon into the salad, add the dressing and toss well. Serve immediately.

mussel and lemon pasta

preparation time **13 mins**
cooking time **17 mins**
total time **30 mins** serves **4**

375 g/12 oz dried spaghetti
1 kg/2 lb mussels
6 tablespoons extra virgin olive oil
2 garlic cloves, sliced
1 large red chilli, deseeded and chopped
grated rind and juice of 1 lemon
4 tablespoons chopped coriander
salt and pepper

one Cook the pasta in a large pan of lightly salted boiling water for 10 minutes, until al dente. Drain and reserve.

two While the pasta is cooking, scrub and debeard the mussels. Discard any that are broken or do not shut immediately when tapped sharply with the back of a knife. Set aside.

three Heat the oil in a wok or large frying pan and fry the garlic, chilli and lemon rind, stirring occasionally, for 3 minutes until golden. Remove from the heat.

four Put the mussels into a large saucepan with 2 tablespoons water, cover tightly, and cook, shaking the pan frequently, for 4 minutes, until the shells have opened. Discard any mussels that remain closed.

five Return the garlic mixture to the heat and stir in the pasta, the mussels and their cooking liquid, lemon juice and coriander. Season to taste with salt and pepper, heat through and serve.

fresh crab and mango salad

preparation time **25 mins**
cooking time **3 mins**
total time **28 mins** serves **4**

1 small egg yolk
1 teaspoon Dijon mustard
1 tablespoon fresh lemon juice
8 tablespoons extra virgin olive oil
250 g/8 oz fresh crab meat
1 red chilli, deseeded and chopped
125 g/4 oz fine green beans
1 small mango
1 head chicory
2 tablespoons chopped coriander
salt and pepper

one Whisk the egg yolk, mustard and lemon juice until frothy and then slowly whisk in 5 tablespoons of the oil. Season to taste with salt and pepper.

two Carefully pick through the crab to remove any small pieces of shell or cartilage. Stir the chilli into the crab meat with the dressing.

three Blanch the beans in lightly salted boiling water for 3 minutes. Drain and refresh under cold water, then pat dry with kitchen paper. Peel the mango and then thinly slice the flesh from the stone. Separate the chicory into spears. Arrange the chicory, mango, beans and crab on serving plates.

four In a food processor or blender, process the remaining oil with the coriander leaves and a little salt to make a fresh green dressing. Pour around the salad and serve.

cucumber and mint refresher

preparation time **7 mins**
total time **7 mins** serves **2**

1 cucumber
2 tablespoons chopped mint
300 ml/½ pint natural yogurt
2 tablespoons rosewater
2 teaspoons clear honey
ice cubes, to serve
mint sprigs, to decorate

one Peel the cucumber and cut it in half lengthways. Scoop out the seeds and chop the flesh roughly. Put the chopped mint inton a blender with the cucumber, yogurt, rosewater and honey. Process until smooth and speckled with green flecks.
two Put some ice cubes into glasses and top up with the cucumber drink. Decorate with mint sprigs.

chilled peach zinger

preparation time **10–12 mins**
total time **10–12 mins** serves **4**

4 ripe peaches
1 tablespoon citrus cordial
juice of 1 lime
crushed ice
300 ml/½ pint lemonade

one Immerse the peaches in boiling water for 1–2 minutes. Refresh in cold water and peel off the skins. Halve, stone and roughly chop the flesh.
two Place the peaches, cordial and lime juice in a food processor or blender and process to a smooth purée.
three Half-fill 4 tall glasses with crushed ice, add the peach purée and top up with lemonade.

Add a measure of vodka during step 2 for an alcoholic version.

mid-week meals

When friends are coming over mid-week, I like to pick up a few fresh ingredients on my way home to add to those in my cupboards and throw together a yummy supper without having to get too stressed by it all. Quite often, with a little organization, I manage to prepare a starter, main course and a pudding in no time at all.

pumpkin and coconut soup

preparation time **10 mins**
cooking time **20 mins**
total time **30 mins** serves **6**

2 tablespoons sunflower oil
1 onion, chopped
4 garlic cloves, crushed
2.5 cm/1 inch piece of fresh root ginger,
    peeled and grated
2 red chillies, deseeded and chopped
1 teaspoon ground coriander
½ teaspoon ground cumin
seeds from 2 cardamom pods
750 g/1½ lb pumpkin, peeled and diced
750 ml/1¼ pints vegetable stock
150 ml/¼ pint coconut milk
1 tablespoon tamarind pulp
1 cinnamon stick, lightly crushed
2 tablespoons chopped coriander
salt and pepper

TO SERVE
coriander leaves
natural yogurt

one Heat the oil in a large saucepan and fry
the onion, garlic, ginger, chillies and spices,
stirring frequently, for 10 minutes.
two Add the pumpkin, stock, coconut milk,
tamarind pulp and cinnamon and bring to the
boil. Lower the heat, cover and simmer
gently for about 10 minutes, just until the
pumpkin is tender. Discard the cinnamon.
three Process the soup with the chopped
coriander in a food processor or blender until
smooth. Transfer the soup to bowls, garnish
with coriander leaves and yogurt and serve.

fresh pea and tomato frittata

preparation time **8 mins**
cooking time **12 mins**
total time **20 mins** serves **4**

125 g/4 oz fresh or frozen peas
2 tablespoons extra virgin olive oil
1 bunch spring onions, sliced
1 garlic clove, crushed
125 g/4 oz cherry tomatoes, halved
6 eggs
2 tablespoons chopped mint
handful pea shoots (optional)
salt and pepper

TO SERVE
rocket leaves
shavings of Parmesan cheese (optional)

one If using fresh peas, cook them in
a pan of lightly salted boiling water for
3 minutes. Drain and refresh under
cold water.
two Heat the oil in a nonstick frying pan
and fry the spring onions and garlic for
2 minutes, then add the tomatoes and peas.
three Beat the eggs with the mint and
season with salt and pepper. Swirl the
egg mixture into the pan, scatter over
the pea shoots and cook over a medium
heat for 3–4 minutes, until almost set.
four Transfer to a preheated grill and cook
for a further 2–3 minutes, until lightly
browned and cooked through. Cool slightly
and serve in wedges with the rocket and
Parmesan shavings, if liked.

A really tasty toasted sandwich. To serve 4, double the quantities opposite. You will probably need to griddle the bread in batches unless you have 2 griddle pans, or grill it in the oven.

sweet potato, olive and fontina panini

preparation time **5 mins**
cooking time **12 mins**
total time **17 mins** serves **2–4**

250 g/8 oz sweet potato, thinly sliced
1 tablespoon extra virgin olive oil
vegetable oil, for frying
12 sage leaves
1 ciabatta
2 tablespoons olive paste
250 g/8 oz Fontina cheese, thinly sliced
salt and pepper
green salad, to serve

one Brush the sweet potato slices with the olive oil and season lightly with salt and pepper. Cook in a hot griddle pan for 3–4 minutes on each side, until charred and tender. Clean the griddle.

two Meanwhile, heat a little vegetable oil in a small frying pan and fry the sage leaves for about 30 seconds, until crisp. Drain on kitchen paper.

three Cut the ciabatta into quarters and then trim these so that all 4 pieces will fit on to the griddle. Heat the griddle and brush with a little oil. Cook the ciabatta pieces, cut-side down, for 1 minute, until toasted.

four Spread the toasted sides of the ciabatta with the olive paste and sandwich them together with layers of cheese, sage leaves and the potato slices.

five Griddle the whole sandwiches for 1–2 minutes each side, until toasted and the cheese in the middle is melting. Serve with a green salad.

chicken, taleggio and parma ham melt

preparation time **10 mins**
cooking time **20 mins**
total time **30 mins** serves **4**

4 skinless chicken breast fillets
4 slices Parma ham
125 g/4 oz Taleggio or Camembert cheese
extra virgin olive oil, for brushing
balsamic vinegar, for drizzling
salt and pepper
tomato, olive and basil salad, to serve

one Using a sharp knife, slice horizontally through the thicker side of the chicken breast fillets without cutting all the way through. Open them out and season with salt and pepper.

two Lay a slice of ham in each breast. Slice the cheese into 4 and add to the ham. Fold the chicken over to enclose the filling.

three Brush each chicken breast with a little olive oil and cook in a hot griddle pan for 8–10 minutes on each side, until browned and cooked through, and the cheese is oozing from the middle.

four Serve the chicken drizzled with a little balsamic vinegar, more olive oil and a tomato, olive and basil salad.

mussels with lemon curry sauce

preparation time **15 mins**
cooking time **15 mins**
total time **30 mins** serves **4**

1 kg/2 lb mussels, scrubbed and debearded
125 ml/4 fl oz Indian lager
25 g/1 oz unsalted butter
1 onion, chopped
1 garlic clove, crushed
2.5 cm/1 inch piece of fresh root ginger,
  peeled and grated
1 tablespoon medium curry powder
150 ml/¼ pint single cream
2 tablespoons lemon juice
salt and pepper
chopped parsley, to garnish
crusty bread, to serve

one Discard any mussels that are broken or do not close immediately when tapped sharply with a knife. Place them in a large pan with the lager, cover and cook, shaking the pan frequently, for 4 minutes, until all the shells have opened. Discard any that remain closed. Strain and reserve the cooking liquid. Keep the mussels warm.
two Meanwhile, melt the butter in a large pan and fry the onion, garlic, ginger and curry powder, stirring frequently, for 5 minutes.
three Strain in the reserved cooking liquid and bring to the boil. Boil until reduced by half. Whisk in the cream and lemon juice and simmer gently.
four Stir in the mussels, warm through and season to taste with salt and pepper. Garnish with chopped parsley and serve with crusty bread.

smoked haddock, poached eggs and caper butter

preparation time **10 mins**
cooking time **10 mins**
total time **20 mins** serves **4**

4 smoked haddock fillets, about
  175 g/6 oz each
4 eggs
125 g/4 oz unsalted butter, softened
2 tablespoons capers in brine, drained
  and rinsed
6 dill sprigs
salt and pepper

one Put the haddock into a frying pan, skin-side up, cover with cold water and bring to the boil. Poach for 5 minutes, then remove with a slotted spoon and drain on kitchen paper. Set aside and keep warm. Reserve the fish cooking liquid.
two Crack the eggs into the cooking liquid and poach for 2–3 minutes.
three Melt the butter in a frying pan until foaming. Add the capers and dill and fry until the butter starts to turn brown. Season to taste with salt and pepper.
four Top each haddock fillet with a poached egg and serve drizzled with the caper butter.

stir-fried beef with noodles

preparation time **20 mins**
cooking time **5 mins**
total time **25 mins** serves **4**

2 tablespoons dark soy sauce
2 teaspoons clear honey
500 g/1 lb thick sirloin steak, very thinly sliced
50 g/2 oz cashew nuts
175 g/6 oz flat rice noodles
2 tablespoons sunflower oil
1 teaspoon sesame oil
1 garlic clove, chopped
1 fresh red chilli, deseeded and chopped
1 red pepper, deseeded and sliced
50 ml/2 fl oz hot beef stock
1 tablespoon Thai fish sauce
2 tablespoons lime juice
4 tablespoons chopped basil

one Combine the soy sauce and honey in a large dish. Add the beef and turn to coat. Set aside to marinate for 10 minutes, then drain the beef, reserving the marinade.
two Meanwhile, toast the cashews, then roughly chop them.
three Soak the noodles according to the packet instructions, then drain and set aside.
four Heat the two oils in a wok, add the garlic, chilli and red pepper and stir-fry for 30 seconds. Add the beef and stir-fry for a further 2 minutes.
five Add the noodles, reserved marinade, beef stock, fish sauce and lime juice and cook for 2 minutes. Sprinkle with the basil and serve topped with the cashews.

garlicky prawn and basil pasta

preparation time **10 mins**
cooking time **12 mins**
total time **22 mins** serves **4**

375 g/12 oz dried fusilli
2 garlic cloves
25 g/1 oz pine nuts
6 tablespoons extra virgin olive oil
a pinch of dried chilli flakes
375 g/12 oz cooked peeled tiger prawns
juice of ½ lemon
25 g/1 oz chopped basil leaves
salt and pepper

one Cook the pasta in a large saucepan of
lightly salted, boiling water for 10–12 minutes
until tender but still firm to the bite. Drain
the pasta, reserving 50 ml/2 fl oz of the
cooking liquid.
two Meanwhile, crush the garlic and toast
the pine nuts. Heat the oil in a wok and
stir-fry the garlic and chilli flakes for about
30 seconds, or until starting to brown. Add
the prawns and stir-fry for 1 minute.
three Stir in the pasta, the reserved cooking
liquid, pine nuts, lemon juice and basil,
season to taste with salt and pepper and
heat through before serving.

pasta with broad beans and artichoke pesto

preparation time **10 mins**
cooking time **12 mins**
total time **22 mins** serves **4**

375 g/12 oz dried penne
375 g/12 oz frozen broad beans
75 g/3 oz marinated charred artichokes,
    roughly chopped
1 garlic clove, chopped
15 g/½ oz parsley, chopped
1 tablespoon pine nuts
15 g/½ oz Pecorino cheese, grated,
    plus extra to serve
150 ml/¼ pint extra virgin olive oil
salt and pepper

one Cook the pasta in a large saucepan of
lightly salted, boiling water for 10–12 minutes,
until tender but still firm to the bite. At the
same time, blanch the broad beans in a pan
of lightly salted, boiling water for 3 minutes.
Drain and set aside.
two Put the artichokes, garlic, parsley and
pine nuts in a food processor and process
until fairly smooth. Transfer the mixture to
a bowl and stir in the Pecorino and oil and
season to taste with salt and pepper.
three Drain the pasta, reserving
4 tablespoons of the cooking liquid, and
return it to the pan. Add the pesto mixture,
broad beans and reserved cooking liquid and
season to taste with pepper. Toss over a
medium heat until warmed through. Serve
with extra grated Pecorino.

spinach and four cheese pizza

preparation time **18 mins**
cooking time **12 mins**
total time **30 mins** serves **4**

280 g/8½ oz packet pizza base mix
1 tablespoon extra virgin olive oil
1 garlic clove, crushed
2 rosemary sprigs, chopped
200 g/7 oz frozen spinach, thawed
125 g/4 oz Dolcelatte cheese
4 tablespoons mascarpone cheese
a pinch of grated nutmeg
150 g/5 oz mozzarella cheese, sliced
25 g/1 oz Parmesan cheese, grated
salt and pepper

one Put two baking sheets into a preheated oven, 220°C (425°F), Gas Mark 7, to heat up.
two Make up the pizza dough with the olive oil, according to the packet instructions, adding the garlic and rosemary to the mix. Divide the dough in half and roll out each piece to a 35 cm/14 inch round.
three Extract all the excess liquid from the spinach. Beat in the Dolcelatte, mascarpone, grated nutmeg, salt and pepper.
four Place one pizza base on a well-floured board and top with half the spinach mixture, half the mozzarella and half the Parmesan. Season with salt and pepper. Carefully slide on to one of the heated baking sheets. Repeat to make the second pizza and slide on to the second baking sheet.
five Bake for 12 minutes, swapping the pizzas half-way through, to brown evenly. To serve, cut each pizza in half.

spring green and goats' cheese risotto

preparation time **8 mins**
cooking time **22 mins**
total time **30 mins** serves **4**

4 tablespoons extra virgin olive oil
2 leeks, sliced
2 garlic cloves, chopped
250 g/8 oz risotto rice
150 ml/¼ pint dry white wine
1.2 litres/2 pints hot vegetable stock
250 g/8 oz broccoli, cut into florets
250 g/8 oz baby spinach, shredded
25 g/1 oz chopped mixed herbs (such as basil, chives, mint and tarragon)
125 g/4 oz soft goats' cheese, mashed
50 g/2 oz Parmesan cheese, grated
salt and pepper

one Heat the oil in a large saucepan and fry the leeks and garlic for 1 minute. Add the rice and stir for 30 seconds, until all the grains are glossy. Add the wine, bring to the boil and cook gently until almost all the liquid has evaporated.
two Gradually add the stock, a ladleful at a time, stirring frequently for 18 minutes until almost all the stock is absorbed. Add the broccoli to the rice after 12 minutes.
three Stir the spinach, herbs and both cheeses into the rice with the remaining stock. Season to taste with salt and pepper and cook for a final 2 minutes until the spinach is wilted. Serve immediately.

pork steaks with apples and mustard mash

preparation time **5 mins**
cooking time **23 mins**
total time **28 mins** serves **4**

4 medium floury potatoes, diced
1 large green apple, peeled, cored
    and quartered
a handful sage leaves, chopped
2 tablespoons extra virgin olive oil
1 tablespoon lemon juice
1 tablespoon clear honey
4 pork steaks, about 200 g/7 oz each
50 g/2 oz butter
2 tablespoons milk
1 tablespoon Dijon mustard
salt and pepper

one Boil the potatoes in lightly salted,
boiling water for 10 minutes, until tender.
two Cut the apple quarters into thick
wedges. Mix the sage with the oil, lemon
juice and honey and season with salt and
pepper. Mix half the flavoured oil with
the apple wedges. Brush the rest over
the pork.
three Grill the steaks for 3–4 minutes on
each side, until browned and cooked
through. Set aside and keep warm.
four Drain the potatoes, mash and beat in
40 g/1½ oz of the butter, the milk and
mustard and season to taste with salt and
pepper. Keep warm.
five Melt the remaining butter in a frying
pan and quickly fry the apple wedges for
2–3 minutes, until golden and softened.
Serve the pork with the mustard mash,
apples and any pork juices.

gammon steaks with creamy lentils

preparation time **8 mins**
cooking time **22 mins**
total time **30 mins** serves **4**

125 g/4 oz Puy lentils
50 g/2 oz butter
2 shallots
1 garlic clove, chopped
2 thyme sprigs, crushed
1 teaspoon cumin seeds
4 teaspoons Dijon mustard
2 teaspoons clear honey
4 gammon steaks
125 ml/4 fl oz dry cider
75 ml/3 fl oz single cream
salt and pepper
thyme leaves, to garnish

one Place the lentils in a pan and cover with
cold water. Bring to the boil and cook for
20 minutes.
two Meanwhile, melt the butter in a frying
pan and fry the shallots, garlic, thyme and
cumin, stirring frequently, for 10 minutes, until
the shallots are soft and golden.
three Blend the mustard and honey and
season to taste with salt and pepper. Brush
the mixture over the gammon steaks and
grill for 3 minutes on each side, until golden
and cooked through. Keep warm.
four Drain the lentils and add to the shallot
mixture. Add the cider, bring to the boil and
cook until reduced to about 4 tablespoons.
Stir in the cream, heat through and season
with salt and pepper. Garnish the gammon
steaks with thyme leaves and serve.

instant apple crumbles

preparation time **7 mins**
cooking time **13 mins**
total time **20 mins** serves **4**

1 kg/2 lb Bramley apples, peeled, cored
   and thickly sliced
25 g/1 oz butter
2 tablespoons caster sugar
1 tablespoon lemon juice
2 tablespoons water
cream or ice cream, to serve

CRUMBLE
50 g/2 oz butter
75 g/3 oz fresh wholemeal breadcrumbs
25 g/1 oz pumpkin seeds
2 tablespoons soft brown sugar

one Place the apples in a saucepan with the
butter, sugar, lemon juice and water. Cover
and simmer for 8–10 minutes, until softened.
two Melt the butter for the crumble in
a frying pan and stir-fry the breadcrumbs
until lightly golden, then add the pumpkin
seeds and stir-fry for a further 1 minute.
Remove from the heat and stir in the sugar.
three Spoon the apple mixture into bowls,
sprinkle with the crumble and serve with
cream or ice cream.

This is not strictly a crumble – the
apples are stewed and then topped
with crispy crumbs and toasted
pumpkin seeds, but it tastes almost
the same as the real thing and is
truly delicious.

bananas with palm sugar toffee sauce

preparation time **2 mins**
cooking time **4 mins**
total time **6 mins** serves **4**

4 bananas
125 g/4 oz unsalted butter
125 g/4 oz palm sugar
125 ml/4 fl oz double cream
dash of lime juice
vanilla ice cream, to serve
ground cinnamon or grated nutmeg,
   to decorate (optional)

one Peel the bananas and cut them into
quarters or in half lengthways. Melt the
butter in a frying pan and fry the banana
halves for about on 30 seconds each side,
until lightly golden. Transfer to a warm dish
with a slotted spoon.
two Stir the sugar and cream into the pan
and heat gently to dissolve the sugar.
Simmer gently for 2–3 minutes, until
thickened. Add lime juice to taste.
three Serve the bananas drizzled with the
toffee sauce and with a scoop of ice cream.
Sprinkle with cinnamon or nutmeg to
decorate, if liked.

two's company

These recipes are perfect for a romantic evening in, or for a tête-à-tête meal. Many cookbooks cater for four to six servings, but I often end up cooking for myself and one friend, so these dishes all serve two. Of course, if you fancy making any of them for more people, simply multiply the ingredients accordingly.

pasta primavera

preparation time **10 mins**
cooking time **15 mins**
total time **25 mins** serves **2**

375 g/12 oz mixed summer vegetables
   (such as baby carrots, fine beans, courgettes
   and fennel)
250 g/8 oz dried spaghetti
2 tablespoons extra virgin olive oil
1 shallot, finely chopped
1 garlic clove, sliced
120 ml/4 fl oz dry white wine
200 ml/7 fl oz single cream
2 tablespoons chopped mixed herbs
   (such as chervil, chives, mint and parsley)
25 g/1 oz Parmesan cheese, grated
salt and pepper

one Trim and slice the vegetables as
necessary and plunge them into a large pan
of lightly salted, boiling water and blanch for
2 minutes. Drain in a sieve, reserving the
cooking liquid, and refresh the vegetables in
cold water.
two Bring the vegetable water back to
the boil, add the pasta and cook for
10–12 minutes, until it is tender but still
firm to the bite. Drain and reserve.
three Meanwhile, heat the oil in a wok or
large frying pan and fry the shallot and garlic
for 5 minutes. Add the vegetables and cook
for a further 1 minute.
four Pour in the wine, bring it to the boil and
cook until reduced by half. Add the cream
and herbs and bring the sauce back to the
boil. Stir in the spaghetti and Parmesan and
season to taste with salt and pepper. Heat
through and serve.

pasta with radicchio and cheese crumbs

preparation time **5 mins**
cooking time **17 mins**
total time **22 mins** serves **2**

175 g/6 oz dried spaghetti
65 g/2½ oz butter
25 g/1 oz fresh white breadcrumbs
15 g/½ oz Parmesan cheese, grated
2 shallots, finely chopped
1 garlic clove, sliced
1 head radicchio, shredded
dash of lemon juice
salt and pepper

one Cook the pasta in a large pan of lightly
salted, boiling water for 10–12 minutes, until
tender but still firm to the bite. Drain the
pasta, reserving 2 tablespoons of the
cooking liquid.
two Meanwhile, melt half the butter in a
frying pan and fry the breadcrumbs, stirring
frequently, for about 5 minutes, until evenly
golden and crisp. Transfer the crumbs to a
bowl, cool slightly and add the Parmesan.
three Heat the remaining butter in a wok or
large saucepan and fry the shallots and
garlic, stirring occasionally, for 5 minutes,
until softened. Add the radicchio with a little
lemon juice and season to taste with salt
and pepper. Stir over a low heat for about
2 minutes, until the radicchio has wilted.
Add the pasta, toss until heated through and
serve topped with the cheese crumbs.

seafood fondue

preparation time **10 mins**
cooking time **20 mins**
total time **30 mins** serves **2**

1 lemon grass stalk, finely shredded
4 lime leaves, finely shredded
2 garlic cloves, chopped
2.5 cm/1 inch piece of fresh root ginger,
    peeled and grated
4 small red chillies, deseeded and chopped
1.2 litres/2 pints fish stock
2 tablespoons Thai fish sauce
1 tablespoon light soy sauce
1 tablespoon palm sugar
juice of 1 lime
125 g/4 oz egg thread noodles
6 large raw prawns, peeled and deveined
    (see page 33)
4 prepared baby squid, sliced into rings
6 prepared scallops
50 g/2 oz bean sprouts
a large handful herb sprigs (such as basil,
    coriander and mint)

This is an Asian seafood dish where
the stock is brought to the table
in a special pot called a steamboat
and the raw ingredients are served
on a platter, so you can poach
them in the stock yourself, much
as you would with a fondue.
You can either use a fondue
pan or buy a steamboat from an
Oriental or good kitchen shop.

one Place the lemon grass, lime leaves,
garlic, ginger, chillies, stock, fish sauce,
soy sauce, sugar and lime juice in a
saucepan. Bring to the boil, cover and
simmer for 20 minutes.

two Meanwhile, soak the noodles in hot
water, according to packet instructions, then
drain and refresh under cold water. Butterfly
the prawns (see page 33), and slice the
squid into rings.

three Transfer the hot stock to a Chinese
steamboat or a fondue pan and light the
burner. Arrange the raw seafood, bean
sprouts, noodles and herbs on a platter and
transport to the table so that each person
can cook their own food in the hot stock.

malay chicken noodles

preparation time **13 mins**
cooking time **12 mins**
total time **25 mins** serves **2**

2 garlic cloves
2 tablespoons sunflower oil
1 fresh red chilli, deseeded and finely chopped
2 shallots, thinly sliced
2 skinless chicken breast fillets, thinly sliced
2.5 cm/1 inch piece of fresh root ginger,
    peeled and grated
¼ teaspoon ground coriander
125 g/4 oz thin rice noodles
50 g/2 oz mangetout, halved
1 red pepper, deseeded and sliced
25 g/1 oz bean sprouts
3 tablespoons kecap manis or soy sauce
1 tablespoon Thai fish sauce
1 tablespoon medium dry sherry
1 tablespoon lemon juice
chopped coriander, to garnish

one Slice 1 garlic clove and crush the other. Heat the oil in a wok and stir-fry the sliced garlic, chilli and shallots for about 3 minutes, until golden and starting to crisp, but do not allow them to burn. Drain with a slotted spoon and reserve. Remove the wok from the heat, reserving the oil.

two Toss together the chicken breast, ginger, crushed garlic and ground coriander in a bowl. Soak the noodles in hot water, according to the packet instructions, then drain and reserve.

three Reheat the oil in the wok and add the chicken mixture. Stir-fry for 3 minutes, until golden. Add the mangetout, red pepper and bean sprouts to the wok, and stir-fry for a further 1 minute.

four Finally, add the noodles, kecap manis or soy sauce, fish sauce, sherry and lemon juice and cook for 1–2 minutes, until heated through. Serve topped with the shallot mixture and chopped coriander.

steamed chicken with pak choi and ginger

preparation time **12 mins**
cooking time **11 mins**
total time **23 mins** serves **2**

1 cm/½ inch piece of fresh root ginger,
    peeled and grated
1 small garlic clove, crushed
1 tablespoon dark soy sauce
1 tablespoon tangerine syrup
1½ teaspoons mirin
1 teaspoon sugar
a pinch of Chinese five-spice powder
2 skinless chicken breast fillets
2 pak choi, halved
coriander sprigs, to garnish

GINGER SALSA
2.5 cm/1 inch piece of stem ginger, peeled
    and very finely shredded
1 red chilli, deseeded and finely chopped
a few coriander leaves, chopped
1 teaspoon sesame oil
juice of ½ lime
salt and pepper

one Combine the ginger, garlic, soy sauce, tangerine syrup, mirin, sugar and five-spice powder in a bowl. Place the chicken in a shallow, heatproof dish, pour in the mixture and turn to coat thoroughly. Set aside to marinate for 10 minutes.

two Meanwhile, make the ginger salsa. Mix together the ginger, chilli, coriander leaves, sesame oil and lime juice and season to taste with salt and pepper.

three Place the chicken with the marinade in a bamboo steamer and cook for 8 minutes. Remove the chicken from the dish and keep warm. Steam the pak choi in the cooking juices for 2–3 minutes. Serve the chicken and pak choi with the salsa, garnished with coriander sprigs.

tea-smoked duck with roasted squash salad

preparation time **10 mins**
cooking time **20 mins**
total time **30 mins** serves **2**

250 g/8 oz butternut squash, peeled and cut
    into cubes
4 teaspoons olive oil
2 small duck breasts, about 200 g/7 oz each
1 teaspoon Thai seven-spice seasoning
1 quantity Smoke Mix (see page 9)
2 star anise
50 g/2 oz frisée lettuce
1 tablespoon wild garlic leaves or chives
salt and pepper

DRESSING
2.5 cm/1 inch piece of fresh root ginger,
    peeled and grated
1 tablespoon rice vinegar
pinch of dried chilli flakes
4 tablespoons sunflower oil

one Toss the squash with 3 teaspoons of
the oil in a roasting tin or ovenproof dish.
Season to taste with salt and pepper.
Transfer to a preheated oven, 220°C (425°F),
Gas Mark 7, and roast for 20 minutes until
the squash is golden.

two Meanwhile, brush the duck breasts
with the remaining oil and rub with
1 teaspoon salt and the seven-spice mix.

three Line a wok with 1–2 sheets of foil,
making sure the foil is touching the base
of the wok. Add the smoke mix and the star
anise, and place a trivet over the top. Lay
the duck breasts on the trivet, cover with a
tight-fitting lid and smoke over a medium
heat for 12 minutes. Remove the wok from
the heat and set aside, still covered, for a
further 5 minutes.

four To make the dressing, mix the ginger,
vinegar, chilli flakes and sunflower oil.

five Put the frisée and wild garlic leaves or
chives into a serving bowl, add the squash
and the dressing and toss to mix. Cut the
duck breasts in half or into slices and serve
with the salad.

sweet bruschetta with sauternes custard

preparation time **5 mins**, plus infusing
cooking time **15 mins**
total time **20 mins** serves **2**

25 g/1 oz unsalted butter
1 egg
few drops vanilla essence
2 tablespoons caster sugar
125 ml/4 fl oz milk
4 slices white bread, crusts removed
raspberries, to serve

SAUTERNES CUSTARD
100 ml/3½ fl oz double cream
2 tablespoons Sauternes or other sweet
    white wine
½ vanilla pod
2 egg yolks
1 tablespoon caster sugar

one First, make the custard. Heat the cream, wine and vanilla pod to boiling point. Remove the pan from the heat and set aside to infuse for 10 minutes.

two Beat together the egg yolks and sugar in a bowl, strain in the infused cream and return to the pan. Heat gently, stirring constantly until thickened. Do not allow the mixture to boil. Remove the pan from the heat and keep warm.

three Melt the butter in a frying pan. Meanwhile, beat the egg with the vanilla essence, sugar and milk in a shallow bowl. Dip in the bread slices and fry in the butter for 1–2 minutes each side, until crisp and lightly golden. Serve topped with raspberries and hand the custard round separately.

This dish reminds me of bread
and butter pudding, but here
it is cooked like French toast,
making it lighter than the more
traditional English baked pudding.

fruit and mascarpone gratin

preparation time **5 mins**
cooking time **3 mins**
total time **8 mins** serves **2**

50 g/2 oz mixed fruits and berries (such
　　as peaches, strawberries, raspberries
　　and blueberries)
50 g/2 oz mascarpone cheese
1 egg yolk
25 g/1 oz caster sugar
1 tablespoon Amaretto di Saronno

one Prepare the fruits and arrange in a
single layer on 2 heatproof plates or in
individual gratin dishes.
two Beat together the mascarpone, egg
yolk, sugar and Amaretto until smooth and
then spoon over the fruits.
three Cook under a preheated grill for about
3 minutes, until the sauce is caramelized
and the fruits are softened.

champagne and raspberry framboise

preparation time **2 mins**, plus chilling
total time **17 mins** serves **2**

25 g/1 oz ripe raspberries
1 tablespoon Framboise
½ bottle chilled Champagne

one Mix the raspberries with the Framboise
and chill for 15 minutes.
two Spoon into cocktail glasses or flutes
and top up with the Champagne.

An ideal Champagne cocktail to
get the evening off to a bubbly start.

This is not a true sorbet, but a cheat's version. Frozen summer
berries are blended with fruit cordial for an instant ice.

summer berry sorbet

preparation time **5 mins**
freezing time **25 mins**
total time **30 mins** serves **2**

250 g/8 oz frozen mixed summer berries
75 ml/3 fl oz spiced berry cordial
2 tablespoons Kirsch
1 tablespoon lime juice

one Put a shallow plastic container into the
freezer to chill. Process the frozen berries,
cordial, Kirsch and lime juice in a food
processor or blender until it becomes a
smooth purée. Be careful not to over-
process the purée as this will soften the
mixture too much.
two Spoon the sorbet into the chilled
container and freeze for at least 25 minutes.
Spoon into bowls and serve.

fruit fritters
with ice cream

preparation time **5 mins**
cooking time **6–8 mins**
total time **11–13 mins** serves **2**

15 g/½ oz unsalted butter
40 g/1½ oz plain flour
a pinch of ground mixed spice
a pinch of salt
1 egg, separated
75 ml/3 fl oz sparkling mineral water
125 g/4 oz fresh fruit
sunflower oil, for deep-frying
caster sugar, for dusting
vanilla ice cream, to serve

one Melt the butter in a small pan. Sift the
flour, spice and salt into a bowl. Beat in the
egg yolk, melted butter and water to make a
fairly smooth batter.
two Whisk the egg white in a separate bowl
and fold into the batter.
three Heat 5 cm/2 inches of oil in a deep
pan. Meanwhile, peel, stone and quarter the
fruit, as necessary.
four Dip the prepared fruit into the batter
and deep-fry for 1–2 minutes, until crisp and
golden. Drain on kitchen paper.
five Dust the fritters with a little caster
sugar and serve with a scoop of ice cream.

outdoor eating

There is definitely something magical about eating al fresco, even if, like me, you have only a small terrace. Barbecues simply epitomize summer evenings and many of the recipes in this chapter are cooked over hot coals. You'll also find several dishes ideal for picnics, so allow the food to cool, then wrap it well and transport as necessary.

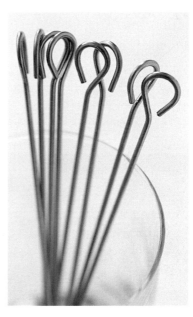

mushroom parcels with melting cheese

preparation time **12–15 mins**
cooking time **15 mins**
total time **27–30 mins** serves **4**

12 flat mushrooms
2 garlic cloves, crushed
1 teaspoon chopped thyme
dash of lemon juice
125 g/4 oz softened butter
50 g/2 oz Pecorino cheese, grated
salt and pepper
crusty bread, to serve

one Divide the mushrooms between
4 large pieces of foil. Beat the garlic, thyme
and lemon juice into the butter and season
to taste with salt and pepper. Dot the
flavoured butter over the mushrooms.
two Seal the foil to form parcels and cook
over hot coals or in a preheated oven, 200°C
(400°F), Gas Mark 6, for 10–15 minutes.
three Open the parcels, sprinkle over the
cheese and allow to melt slightly then serve
with crusty bread.

indian spiced pumpkin wedges with coconut pesto

preparation time **10 mins**
cooking time **12–14 mins**
total time **22–24 mins** serves **4**

1 teaspoon cumin seeds
1 teaspoon coriander seeds
2 cardamom pods
1 kg/2 lb pumpkin, cut into wedges
   1 cm/½ inch thick
3 tablespoons sunflower oil
1 teaspoon caster sugar

COCONUT PESTO
25 g/1 oz coriander leaves
1 garlic clove, crushed
1 green chilli, deseeded and chopped
pinch of sugar
1 tablespoon shelled pistachio nuts,
   roughly chopped
6 tablespoons coconut cream
1 tablespoon lime juice
salt and pepper

one Dry-fry the whole spices until browned,
then grind to a powder in a spice grinder.
Place the pumpkin wedges in a dish.
Toss with the oil, sugar and spice mix
to coat.
two Cook the wedges on a barbecue or
under a preheated grill for 6–8 minutes on
each side, until charred and tender.
three Meanwhile, make the pesto. Work
the coriander, garlic, chilli, sugar, nuts and
salt and pepper in a food processor until
fairly finely ground. Add the coconut cream
and lime juice and process again. Transfer
to a bowl and serve with the pumpkin.

Creamy coconut pesto makes a perfect foil to the soft, nutty
wedges of barbecued pumpkin dusted with curry spices.

lemon and herb barbecued chicken wings

preparation time **5 mins**
cooking time **15–20 mins**
total time **20–25 mins** serves **4**

2 garlic cloves, crushed
grated rind and juice of 1 lemon
4 thyme sprigs
6 tablespoons extra virgin olive oil
1 tablespoon clear honey
1 teaspoon dried oregano
1 teaspoon ground cumin
12 chicken wings
salt and pepper

one Place the garlic, lemon rind and juice in a medium bowl. Add the thyme leaves, oil, honey, oregano and cumin and season to taste with salt and pepper.
two Add the chicken wings and stir until they are well coated with the marinade.
three Barbecue or grill the chicken wings for 15–20 minutes, turning and basting until charred and cooked through.

smoked ham and brie frittata

preparation time **4 mins**
cooking time **6 mins**
total time **10 mins**, plus cooling serves **4**

6 large free-range eggs
2 tablespoons chopped parsley
2 tablespoons extra virgin olive oil
125 g/4 oz piece smoked ham or gammon
75 g/3 oz Brie cheese
salt and pepper
tomato salad, to serve

one Beat together the eggs and parsley and season to taste with salt and pepper. Heat the oil in a nonstick frying pan and swirl in the egg mixture.
two Cook the eggs over a medium heat for 3 minutes, until almost set. Meanwhile, shred the ham and thinly slice the Brie.
three Scatter the ham and cheese over the frittata and cook under a preheated grill for 2–3 minutes, until golden and set. Allow to cool slightly and serve with a tomato salad.

aubergine steaks with miso

preparation time **5 mins**, plus marinating
cooking time **6–8 mins**
total time **26–28 mins** serves **2–4**

2 medium aubergines
1 tablespoon groundnut oil
1 tablespoon dark soy sauce,
    plus extra to serve
1 tablespoon balsamic vinegar
1 tablespoon wholegrain barley miso
1 teaspoon stem ginger syrup
    (from a jar)
green salad with sesame seeds,
    to serve

one Cut the aubergines lengthways into
5 mm/¹/₄ inch thick slices. Combine the oil,
soy sauce, vinegar, miso and ginger syrup
and brush all over the aubergines. Set aside
to marinate for 15 minutes.

two Barbecue or grill the aubergines,
basting them frequently with the marinade,
for 2–4 minutes on each side, until they are
charred and tender. Serve the aubergines
with a little extra soy sauce for dipping and
accompanied by a green salad scattered
with sesame seeds.

salt-crusted prawns with chilli jam

preparation time **10 mins**
cooking time **20 mins**
total time **30 mins** serves **4**

12 large raw tiger prawns in their shells
1 tablespoon olive oil
50 g/2 oz sea salt
lemon wedges, to garnish

CHILLI JAM
4 ripe tomatoes
½ red onion
2 red chillies
2 tablespoons dark soy sauce
2 tablespoons clear honey
salt and pepper

one First make the chilli jam. Roughly chop the tomatoes, onion and chillies. Place in a food processor with the soy sauce and honey, season to taste with salt and pepper and process until smooth.
two Transfer the jam to a saucepan and bring to the boil. Simmer rapidly for 15 minutes, until thickened. Plunge the pan into iced water and leave to cool.
three Meanwhile, carefully cut along the back of the prawns with a small pair of scissors and pull out the black vein. Wash and dry well on kitchen paper.
four Toss the prawns with the oil and then coat thoroughly with salt. Cook the prawns in their salt jackets over hot coals or in a heated griddle pan for 2–3 minutes on each side. Serve with the chilli jam and lemon wedges to garnish.

watermelon and feta salad

preparation time **10 mins**
total time **10 mins** serves **4** as a starter

1 tablespoon black sesame seeds
500 g/1 lb watermelon, peeled and diced
175 g/6 oz feta cheese, diced
50 g/2 oz rocket leaves
a few mint, parsley and coriander sprigs
6 tablespoons extra virgin olive oil
1 tablespoon orange flower water
1½ tablespoons lemon juice
1 teaspoon pomegranate syrup (optional)
½ teaspoon sugar
salt and pepper
toasted pitta bread, to serve

one Dry-fry the sesame seeds for a few minutes until aromatic, then set aside.
two Arrange the watermelon and feta on a large plate with the rocket and herbs.
three Whisk together the olive oil, orange flower water, lemon juice, pomegranate syrup, if using, and sugar, then season to taste with salt and pepper and drizzle over the salad. Scatter over the sesame seeds and serve with toasted pitta bread.

A salt crust coats the shells of the prawns as they cook
over hot coals, leaving the flesh inside succulent and sweet.
Peel the salt crust and the shells will come away too.

The combination of hot grilled chicken and cold noodles is exquisite.

chicken teriyaki with soba noodles

preparation time **5 mins**, plus marinating
cooking time **5 mins**
total time **25 mins** serves **4**

4 skinless chicken breast fillets
4 tablespoons dark soy sauce,
　plus extra, to serve
4 tablespoons mirin
2 tablespoons caster sugar
250 g/8 oz soba noodles
sesame oil, to serve

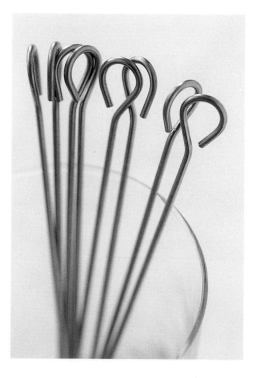

one Cut the chicken breast fillets into
2.5 cm/1 inch cubes and place in a shallow
dish. Combine the soy sauce, mirin and
sugar, add to the chicken and toss well to
coat. Set aside to marinate for 15 minutes.
two Meanwhile, cook the noodles according
to the packet instructions, then drain,
refresh in iced water, drain again and chill.
three Thread the chicken cubes on to metal
skewers and barbecue or grill for 2–3
minutes on each side.
four Toss the noodles with a little sesame
oil and serve with the chicken and extra
sesame oil and soy sauce.

lamb cutlets with anchovies, rosemary and lemon

preparation time **5 mins**, plus marinating
cooking time **6–10 mins**
total time **26–30 mins** serves **4**

juice and finely grated rind of ½ lemon
2 garlic cloves, crushed
4 rosemary sprigs, finely chopped
4 anchovy fillets in oil, drained and
  finely chopped
2 tablespoons extra virgin olive oil
2 tablespoons lemon cordial
12 lamb cutlets
salt and pepper
Sweet Potato Skins (see below), to serve

one Put the lemon rind and juice into a bowl
and add the garlic, rosemary, anchovies,
olive oil and lemon cordial. Mix thoroughly
and add the lamb cutlets. Season with salt
and pepper, turn to coat and set aside to
marinate for 15 minutes.
two Barbecue or grill the lamb cutlets for
3–5 minutes on each side, until charred and
cooked through. Leave to rest for a few
minutes and serve with barbecued sweet
potato skins.

To prepare sweet potato skins, cut baked
sweet potatoes into quarters, scoop out
some of the flesh and brush the skins with
oil. Season to taste with salt and pepper
and barbecue until crisp.

chilli steak baguette

preparation time **5 mins**, plus marinating
cooking time **1 min**
total time **21 mins** serves **4**

2 teaspoons chilli sauce
1 teaspoon clear honey
1 teaspoon sesame oil
4–8 frying steaks, depending on the size
1 large baguette
salt and pepper

SESAME MAYONNAISE
½ teaspoon sesame seeds
1 garlic clove, crushed
1 egg yolk
1–2 teaspoons lime juice
125 ml/4 fl oz safflower oil
1 tablespoon toasted sesame oil

one Combine the chilli sauce, honey, sesame
oil, salt and pepper in a small bowl. Rub the
mixture over the steaks and set aside to
marinate for 15 minutes.
two Meanwhile, make the mayonnaise. Dry-
fry the sesame seeds and set aside to cool.
Put the garlic, egg yolk and 1 teaspoon of
the lime juice into a food processor.
three Process briefly and then, with the
motor running, add the oil steadily through
the funnel until the sauce has thickened.
Season to taste with salt and pepper, stir in
the sesame seeds and add a little more lime
juice, if wished.
four Barbecue, grill or griddle the steaks for
30 seconds on each side. Cut the baguette
into 4, slice the steaks and sandwich into
the baguette quarters with the mayonnaise.
Serve immediately.

prawns and coconut rice

preparation time **10 mins**
cooking time **15 mins**
total time **25 mins** serves **4**

4 tablespoons groundnut oil
250 g/8 oz Thai fragrant rice
1 teaspoon cumin seeds
1 small cinnamon stick
4 lime leaves
400 ml/14 fl oz can coconut milk
150 ml/¼ pint water
1 teaspoon salt
2 garlic cloves, crushed
2.5 cm/1 inch piece of fresh root ginger,
    peeled and grated
pinch of dried chilli flakes
500 g/1 lb raw tiger prawns, peeled and
    deveined (see page 33)
2 tablespoons Thai fish sauce
1 tablespoon lime juice
2 tablespoons chopped coriander
25 g/1 oz dry-roasted peanuts, chopped,
to garnish

one Heat half the oil in a saucepan and
stir-fry the rice until all the grains are glossy.
Add the cumin seeds, cinnamon stick, lime
leaves, coconut milk, water and salt. Bring
to the boil and simmer gently over a low
heat for 10 minutes. Remove from the heat,
cover and leave to rest for 10 minutes.
two Meanwhile, heat the remaining oil in
a wok and stir-fry the garlic, ginger and
chilli flakes for 30 seconds. Add the
prawns and stir-fry for 3–4 minutes, until
just cooked.
three Stir in the coconut rice with the fish
sauce, lime juice and coriander and serve
scattered with the peanuts.

warm ravioli salad with beetroot and bitter leaves

preparation time **10 mins**
cooking time **12 mins**
total time **22 mins** serves **4**

4 tablespoons extra virgin olive oil
2 red onions, thinly sliced
2 garlic cloves, thinly sliced
500 g/1 lb fresh spinach and ricotta ravioli
375 g/12 oz cooked beetroot in natural juices,
    drained and diced
2 tablespoons capers in brine, drained
    and rinsed
2 tablespoons balsamic vinegar
a few mixed bitter salad leaves (such as chicory,
    radicchio, rocket and frisée)
parsley sprigs
basil leaves
salt
Pecorino cheese shavings, to serve (optional)

one Heat 1 tablespoon of the oil in a large
pan and fry the onions and garlic over a
medium heat for 10 minutes, until golden.
two Meanwhile, cook the pasta in a pan of
lightly salted boiling water, for 3 minutes,
until it is tender but still firm to the bite.
Drain and toss with the remaining oil.
three Add the beetroot to the onions with
the capers and vinegar and heat through.
Stir into the ravioli and transfer to a large
bowl to cool for 5 minutes, gathering in all
the juices from the pan.
four Arrange the ravioli in bowls or on plates
with the salad leaves and herbs. Serve
topped with Pecorino shavings, if liked.

Buy the filled pasta from a store that you know sells high-quality fresh pasta. You can vary the filling as preferred.

melon with raspberries and monbazillac

preparation time **2 mins**, plus chilling
total time **17 mins**   serves **4**

2 baby Charentais or cantaloupe melons
125 g/4 oz raspberries
300 ml/½ pint chilled Monbazillac or other
   sweet white wine

one Cut the melons in half and scoop out the seeds. Spoon the raspberries into the hollows and top up with the dessert wine. Chill for at least 15 minutes before serving.

The success of this recipe depends solely on the quality of the fresh fruit, so buy melons with a heavy scent, that feel firm but with a slight give when pressed at the ends.

blueberry fool

preparation time **5 mins**, plus cooling
cooking time **4 mins**
total time **19 mins** serves **4**

250 g/8 oz blueberries
strip of lemon rind
25 g/1 oz caster sugar
juice of ½ lemon
300 ml/½ pint double cream
Quick Hazelnut Melts (see page 22) or dessert
    biscuits, to serve

one Put the blueberries, lemon rind and sugar in a pan and heat gently until the blueberries soften slightly. Plunge the base of the pan into iced water to cool.

two Set aside 4 tablespoons of the blueberries and transfer the rest to a food processor or blender, then add the lemon juice and process until a smooth purée is reached. Whip the cream until it starts to form peaks and fold in all the purée. Spoon into glasses, top with the reserved blueberries and serve with hazelnut melts or dessert biscuits.

barbecued fruits with palm sugar

preparation time **10 mins**, plus cooling
cooking time **3–4 mins** each side on barbecue,
   6–8 mins each side under the grill
total time **18–26 mins** serves **4**

25 g/1 oz palm sugar
grated rind and juice of 1 lime
2 tablespoons water
½ teaspoon cracked black peppercorns
500 g/1 lb mixed prepared fruits (such
   as pineapple slices, mango wedges, and
   peaches)

TO SERVE
cinnamon or vanilla ice cream
lime slices

one Warm the sugar, lime rind and juice, water and peppercorns in a small pan until the sugar has dissolved. Plunge the base of the pan into iced water to cool.

two Brush the cooled syrup over the prepared fruits and barbecue or grill until they are charred and tender. Serve with scoops of cinnamon or vanilla ice cream and slices of lime.

party time

If you think preparing canapés and cocktails for large groups is too time-consuming and not really worth it, then think again. All the dishes in this chapter are quick and easy to prepare and cook, so you can spend more time socializing with your friends than slaving over the proverbial hot stove.

tuna and salsa verde toasts

preparation time **10 mins**
cooking time **10 mins**
total time **20 mins** makes **12**

1 large baguette
2 tablespoons extra virgin olive oil
250 g/8 oz tuna steak
salt and pepper

SALSA VERDE
15 g/½ oz parsley
2 tablespoons chopped mixed herbs (such as
    basil, chives and mint)
1 garlic clove, crushed
15 g/½ oz pitted green olives, chopped
2 anchovy fillets in oil, drained and chopped
½ teaspoon Dijon mustard
1 teaspoon white wine vinegar
50 ml/2 fl oz extra virgin olive oil

one Thinly slice the baguette and brush
with some of the oil. Bake in a preheated
oven, 200°C (400°F), Gas Mark 6, for
8 minutes, until crisp and golden. Leave
to cool.
two Meanwhile, brush the tuna steak with
a little oil, season to taste with salt and
pepper and sear in a hot griddle pan for
30 seconds on each side. Transfer to a
plate and set aside to cool. (The tuna
should be cooked on the outside, while
still raw inside.)
three To make the salsa verde, put the
parsley, mixed herbs, garlic, olives and
anchovies into a food processor or blender.
Add the mustard, vinegar and oil. Process
to a purée and season with salt and pepper.
four Dice the tuna and arrange on top of the
toast with a little of the salsa verde.

quails' eggs with spiced salt

preparation time **5 mins**
cooking time **3 mins**
total time **8 mins** serves **12**

24 quails' eggs
1 teaspoon Szechuan peppercorns
2 tablespoons sea salt
½ teaspoon Chinese five-spice powder

one Cook the eggs in a pan of gently
simmering water for 3 minutes. Plunge
them into cold water.
two Dry-fry the peppercorns until they are
smoking. Cool and grind to a powder with
the salt. Stir in the five-spice powder.
three Peel the eggs and serve with a bowl
of the spiced salt, to dip.

Szechuan peppercorns, also known as farchiew and
anise pepper, are not really pepper, but the dried
red berries of a type of ash tree. Nevertheless, they
have a hot, peppery flavour, which is best brought
out by dry-frying.

chilli crab tartlets

preparation time **12 mins**
total time **12 mins** makes **24** canapés

125 g/4 oz fresh white crab meat
1 ripe tomato, skinned, deseeded and
    finely chopped
1 small garlic clove, crushed
2 tablespoons chopped coriander
¼–½ teaspoon ground cayenne
4 tablespoons mayonnaise
a dash of lemon juice
24 cocktail tartlet cases
salt and pepper

one Put the crab meat in a medium bowl and carefully fork through to remove any small pieces of cartilage that may remain.
two Add the tomato, garlic, coriander, cayenne and mayonnaise to the crab. Stir in a little lemon juice and season to taste with salt and pepper.
three Fill the cocktail tartlet cases with the crab mixture and serve.

open sushi

preparation time **5 mins**
cooking time **15 mins**, plus cooling
total time **30 mins** makes **24** canapés

125 g/4 oz sushi rice
1½ tablespoons rice wine vinegar
1 tablespoon caster sugar
1 teaspoons salt
2 large sheets nori seaweed
50 g/2 oz salmon fillet
about 2 tablespoons wasabi
12 cooked peeled prawns
a few salmon eggs
pickled ginger (optional)
soy sauce, for dipping

one Cook the rice according to the instructions
on the packet. Drain well and immediately stir
in the vinegar, sugar and salt. Transfer to a
bowl set in iced water and allow to cool for
10 minutes.
two Meanwhile, cut the nori sheets in half and
then cut each half into six rectangles, to make
24 in total. Cut the salmon into small dice.
three Dot wasabi in the middle of each piece
of nori, mound a spoonful of rice over this and
top half the canapés with the salmon and half
with the prawns and salmon eggs. Add a sliver
of ginger, if wished, and pull the edges of the
nori up at each side.
four Arrange the sushi on a large platter and
hand them around with a bowl of soy sauce
for dipping.

Wasabi is a fiercely hot, green
Japanese horseradish. It is available
as a paste, or a powder to which
water is added.

sweetcorn cakes with chilli jam

preparation time **25 mins**, including making
the chilli jam
cooking time **2 mins** per batch
total time **29 mins** makes about **24**

1 quantity Chilli Jam (see page 74)
4 lime leaves, very thinly shredded
65 g/2½ oz self-raising flour
1 egg
1 tablespoon Thai fish sauce
1 tablespoon lime juice
150 g/5 oz sweetcorn kernels
24 chicory spears, about 2 heads
vegetable oil, for deep-frying
a few basil, mint and coriander sprigs,
to garnish

one First make the chilli jam. Meanwhile,
place the lime leaves, flour, egg, Thai fish
sauce, lime juice and half the sweetcorn in
a food processor or blender and process
until fairly smooth.
two Transfer the puréed mixture to a bowl
and stir in the remaining sweetcorn. Heat
5 cm/2 inches oil in a wok and deep-fry
teaspoons of the batter, in batches, for
1–2 minutes, until golden. Drain the cakes
on kitchen paper and keep them warm while
you are cooking the remainder.
three Place a sweetcorn cake in each
chicory spear, top with chilli jam and some
fresh herbs and serve immediately.

tandoori chicken poppadums

preparation time **20 mins**, including marinating
 and cooling
cooking time **8 mins**
total time **28 mins** makes **20** canapés

2 skinless chicken breast fillets
1 small garlic clove, crushed
2.5 cm/1 inch piece of fresh root ginger,
 peeled and grated
50 ml/2 fl oz Greek yogurt
1 teaspoon clear honey
1 teaspoon tandoori spice powder
1 teaspoon salt
½ quantity Coconut Pesto (see page 70)
20 mini poppadums

TO SERVE
mango chutney
coriander sprigs

one Score the chicken fillets several times
with a sharp knife and place in a shallow
bowl. Add the garlic, ginger, yogurt, honey,
tandoori spice powder and salt. Toss well
and set aside to marinate for 10 minutes.
two Grill or griddle the marinated chicken
for 3–4 minutes on each side then leave to
cool for about 5 minutes.
three Meanwhile, make the coconut pesto.
Slice the chicken and serve on the
poppadums with a spoonful each of the
pesto and mango chutney and garnish with
a coriander sprig.

Mini poppadums can be found
in most large supermarkets.
If they are unavailable, use large
poppadums and carefully break
them into bite-sized pieces.

smoked trout and avocado blinis

preparation time **13 mins**
cooking time **1–2 mins**
total time **15 mins** makes **24** canapés

½ avocado, peeled, pitted and finely diced
1 spring onion, thinly sliced
1 small garlic clove, crushed
1 tablespoon chopped dill
1 teaspoon lime juice
2 tablespoons crème fraîche
175 g/6 oz smoked trout fillets
24 cocktail blinis
salt and pepper
dill sprigs, to garnish

one Mix together the avocado, spring onion, garlic, dill, lime juice and crème fraîche and season to taste with salt and pepper.
two Flake the trout fillets into bite-sized pieces. Toast the blinis according to the packet instructions and top each one with some avocado cream and trout. Garnish with dill sprigs and serve.

crackling fish parcels

preparation time **17 mins**
cooking time **2–4 mins** per batch
total time **29 mins** makes **12** parcels

1 garlic clove, crushed
1 cm/½ inch piece of fresh root ginger, peeled
  and grated
2 tablespoons finely chopped mint
1 tablespoon sweet chilli sauce
250 g/8 oz skinless salmon fillets
12 small sheets rice flour pancakes
sunflower oil, for frying
salt and pepper

DIPPING SAUCE
2 tablespoons light soy sauce
2 tablespoons mirin
4 tablespoons water
2 tablespoons palm sugar
½ teaspoon dried chilli flakes

one Place all the sauce ingredients in a
small saucepan and heat gently to dissolve
the sugar. Remove from the heat and set
aside to cool.
two Meanwhile, mix together the garlic,
ginger, mint and chilli sauce. Cut the salmon
into 12 equal-sized pieces and coat them
with the spice paste.
three Soak the rice flour pancakes according
to the packet instructions. Place a piece of
salmon fillet on each one, dampen the
edges and fold the pancake over and around
the fish.
four Heat the oil and fry the parcels, in
batches, for 1–2 minutes on each side, until
golden and crisp. Leave to rest for a few
minutes then serve with the dipping sauce.

Rice flour pancakes are wrapped
around small fillets of spiced salmon
and fried until crisp and golden.

sweet wonton mille-feuilles

preparation time **8 mins**, plus cooling
cooking time **3 mins**
total time **21 mins** makes **12**

25 g/1 oz unsalted butter
2 tablespoons caster sugar
½ teaspoon ground cinnamon
9 wonton wrappers
125 g/4 oz mascarpone cheese
1–2 tablespoons icing sugar, plus extra,
    for dusting
1 teaspoon lemon juice
125 g/4 oz strawberries, hulled and sliced

one Melt the butter and mix together the caster sugar and cinnamon. Cut the wonton wrappers into quarters, brush them with the melted butter and coat with a layer of the spiced sugar.

two Place on a baking sheet and bake in a preheated oven, 200°C (400°F), Gas Mark 6, for 2–3 minutes, until crisp and golden. Transfer to a wire rack to cool.

three Beat the mascarpone with the icing sugar and lemon juice and spread a little over 12 of the crisp wontons. Top with half of the strawberry slices. Repeat the process with the remaining mascarpone and strawberries for the second layer. Place the remaining wontons on top and dust with a little extra icing sugar. Serve with glasses of Champagne, if liked.

peach and elderflower bellini

preparation time **6 mins**
total time **6 mins** serves **6**

2 ripe peaches
4 tablespoons elderflower cordial
1 bottle chilled Champagne
a few elderflowers, to garnish (optional)

one Plunge the peaches into boiling water for 1–2 minutes. Refresh under cold water and peel off the skins. Halve, stone and roughly chop the flesh.

two Put the elderflower cordial and peaches in a food processor and process to a fairly smooth purée. Divide the purée between 6 glasses. Top up with Champagne and serve decorated with elderflowers, if liked.

iced lemon and mint vodka

preparation time **6 mins**
total time **6 mins** serves **6**

4 tablespoons lemon juice
8 tablespoons lemon cordial
125 ml/4 fl oz vodka, chilled
ice cubes
a few mint sprigs
tonic water

one Pour the lemon juice, cordial and vodka
into a cocktail shaker and shake well.
two Pour the cocktail into 6 tall glasses
half-filled with ice cubes. Add a few mint
sprigs and top up with tonic water. Serve
immediately.

champagne with pomegranate syrup

preparation time **5 mins**
total time **5 mins** serves **6**

1 small pomegranate
6 teaspoons pomegranate syrup or grenadine
1 bottle chilled Champagne

one Halve the pomegranate and scoop
the seeds into a sieve. Using a wooden
spoon, crush the seeds to extract about
6 tablespoons of juice.
two Put a teaspoonful of pomegranate
syrup or grenadine into the bottom of each
of 6 glasses, top up with Champagne, stir
to dissolve the syrup and add a little of the
pomegranate juice. Serve immediately.

posh nosh

Just because you are entertaining for a formal occasion, there is no need to spend days preparing the food. Nor do you need to worry about the flavour of the dishes being compromised by the length of time taken to make them. All the following recipes are inspiring and delicious, so you can show off your skills without spending your whole day in preparation.

Shucking is the term given to opening oysters. It is best done by the fishmonger, but ask him to reserve any juices.

steamed oysters with asian flavours

preparation time **10 mins**
cooking time **2 mins**
total time **12 mins** serves **4**

12 oysters, shucked
2 spring onions, white parts only, thinly sliced
1.5 cm/¾ inch piece of fresh root ginger,
   peeled and grated
1 small garlic clove, thinly sliced
1 small red chilli, deseeded and sliced
50 ml/2 fl oz sake
2 tablespoons rice vinegar
2 teaspoons dark soy sauce
coriander leaves, to garnish

one Remove the top shell from the shucked oysters and strain the juices through a fine sieve into a small pan. Carefully wipe out any grit that may still remain in the shells.
two Add the spring onions, ginger, garlic, chilli, sake, vinegar and soy sauce to the oyster juices. Warm through gently.
three Arrange the oysters in a large bamboo steamer, cover and steam for 2 minutes. Transfer to plates, spoon over the sauce and serve garnished with coriander leaves.

salt and pepper squid

preparation time **15 mins**, including cooling
cooking time **2 mins** per batch
total time **23–25 mins** serves **4**

750 g/1½ lb prepared squid
4 tablespoons plain flour
1 tablespoon sea salt
2 teaspoons white pepper
pinch of Chinese five-spice powder
vegetable oil, for deep-frying
lime wedges, to serve

CHILLI DIPPING SAUCE
½ small onion, finely chopped
1 garlic clove, finely chopped
1 tablespoon kecap manis
1 tablespoon dark soy sauce
1 teaspoons brown sugar
1 teaspoon sesame oil

one First, make the chilli dipping sauce.
Mix all the ingredients in a small saucepan
and simmer for 8–10 minutes, until reduced
and thickened. Plunge the pan into cold
water to cool the sauce.
two Slice the prepared squid into rings.
Sift the flour, salt, pepper and five-spice
powder into a bowl.
three Dip the squid pieces into the spiced
flour and deep-fry in hot oil, in batches if
necessary, for 1–2 minutes, until crisp.
Drain on kitchen paper and keep warm.
Serve with the dipping sauce.

thai prawn and papaya salad

preparation time **15 mins**, including cooling
total time **15 mins** serves **4** as a starter

1 small green papaya, peeled, deseeded
   and thinly shredded
1 red onion, thinly sliced
1 garlic clove, sliced
2–4 small red chillies, deseeded and
   thinly sliced
1.5 cm/¾ inch piece of fresh root ginger,
   peeled and cut into thin strips
small bunch of coriander, chopped
250 g/8 oz cooked peeled tiger prawns,
   deveined (see page 33)

DRESSING
3 tablespoons palm sugar
2½ tablespoons rice vinegar
2½ tablespoons lime juice
½ teaspoon salt

one First, make the dressing. Put all the
ingredients into a small saucepan and warm
through for just long enough to dissolve the
sugar. Plunge the pan into iced water and
set aside to cool.
two Mix together the papaya, onion, garlic,
chillies, ginger and coriander in a large bowl.
Stir in the tiger prawns and the cooled
dressing and serve.

scallops with ginger and asparagus

preparation time **10 mins**
cooking time **10 mins**
total time **20 mins** serves **4**

12 fresh scallops
2 spring onions, thinly sliced
finely grated rind of 1 lime
1 tablespoon ginger cordial
2 tablespoons extra virgin olive oil, plus
    extra for drizzling
250 g/8 oz thin asparagus spears
juice of ½ lime
a few mixed salad leaves
a few chervil sprigs, to garnish
salt and pepper

one Discard the coral and the tough muscle from the side of each scallop. Wash the scallops and pat dry. Cut each one in half and place in a bowl.

two Mix together the spring onions, lime rind, ginger cordial and half the oil and season to taste with salt and pepper. Pour this dressing over the scallops and set aside to marinate for 15 minutes.

three Meanwhile, steam the asparagus spears for 5–8 minutes, until tender. Toss them with the remaining oil and the lime juice. Season to taste with salt and pepper and keep warm.

four Heat a large nonstick frying pan until hot, add the scallops and fry for 1 minute on each side, until golden and just cooked through. Add the marinade juices.

five Arrange the asparagus spears, salad leaves and chervil on plates with the scallops and any pan juices and serve.

Choose thick fillets of cod from the head end of the fish.

blackened cod with orange and tomato salsa

preparation time **15 mins**
cooking time **8 mins**, plus resting
total time **28 mins** serves **4**

1 large orange
1 garlic clove, crushed
2 large tomatoes, skinned, deseeded and diced
2 tablespoons chopped basil
50 g/2 oz pitted black olives, chopped
5 tablespoons extra virgin olive oil
4 cod fillets, about 175 g/6 oz each
1 tablespoon jerk seasoning
salt and pepper
basil leaves, to garnish
a green salad, to serve (optional)

one Peel and segment the orange, holding it over a bowl to catch the juices. Halve the segments. Mix them with the garlic, tomatoes, basil, olives and 4 tablespoons of the oil, season to taste with salt and pepper and set aside to infuse.

two Wash and pat dry the fish and pull out any small bones with a pair of tweezers. Brush with the remaining oil and coat well with the jerk seasoning.

three Heat a large heavy-based pan and fry the cod fillets, skin-side down, for 5 minutes. Turn them over and cook for a further 3 minutes. Transfer to a low oven, 150°C (300°F), Gas Mark 2, to rest for about 5 minutes.

four Garnish the fish with basil and serve with the salsa and a green salad, if liked.

poached fish in miso

preparation time **5 mins**
cooking time **20 mins**
total time **25 mins** serves **4**

250 g/8 oz Thai fragrant rice
400 ml/14 fl oz fish stock
1 tablespoon dark soy sauce
1 tablespoon mirin
½ tablespoon brown rice vinegar
½ tablespoon barley miso
1 star anise
1 tablespoon sunflower oil
4 salmon fillets, about 150 g/5 oz each
2 teaspoons black sesame seeds
salt and pepper
steamed Chinese leaves, to serve

one Cook the rice according to the packet instructions and keep it warm.

two Put the stock, soy sauce, mirin, vinegar, miso and star anise into a saucepan and bring to the boil, then cover the pan and simmer for 5 minutes.

three Heat the oil in a frying pan and sear the salmon fillets for 1 minute on each side. Transfer them to the stock, then remove the pan from the heat, but leave the salmon fillets to poach in the hot stock for 1 minute.

four Stir the sesame seeds into the cooked rice and spoon into soup plates. Top with the poached salmon and pour in the stock. Serve immediately with steamed Chinese leaves.

duck breast with glazed quince

preparation time **5 mins**
cooking time **20 mins**
total time **25 mins** serves **4**

4 duck breast fillets, about 250 g/8 oz each
1 teaspoon salt
1 medium quince, peeled, cored and cut
    into wedges
2 tablespoons quince paste or honey
150 ml/¼ pint red wine
200 ml/7 fl oz chicken stock
Creamy Mashed Potato, to serve (see below)

one Score the duck skin with several slashes
and rub all over with salt. Dry-fry the fillets,
skin-side down, in a hot pan for 6 minutes
then turn them over and cook for a further
3 minutes. Remove from the pan and
keep warm.
two Discard all but 1 tablespoon of the duck
fat. Add the quince and brown quickly. Stir in
the quince paste and wine and bring to the
boil. Simmer until the quince is tender.
three Remove the quince with a slotted
spoon and keep warm. Add the stock to the
pan and boil until slightly reduced. Slice the
duck and serve with the glazed quince, the
pan juices and creamy mashed potato.

To make creamy mashed potato, cook
and mash the potatoes in the usual way,
but beat in 4–6 tablespoons double
cream with the butter, salt and pepper.

summer pasta of courgettes and dill

preparation time **10 mins**
cooking time **3–5 mins**
total time **15 mins** serves **4**

8 tablespoons extra virgin olive oil
4 garlic cloves, sliced
4 courgettes
4 courgette flowers (optional)
4 tablespoons chopped dill
500 g/1 lb fresh tagliatelle
dash of lemon juice
salt and pepper
freshly grated Parmesan cheese, to serve

one Heat the oil, add the garlic and fry for
1–2 minutes, until lightly golden. Remove
the pan from the heat and set aside.
Coarsely grate the courgettes and thinly
slice the flowers, if using.
two Meanwhile, cook the tagliatelle in a
large pan of lightly salted, boiling water for
3 minutes, until tender but still firm to the
bite. Drain well and return to the pan.
three Immediately stir in the garlic and oil,
courgettes, courgette flowers, if using, and
dill. Season to taste with lemon juice, salt
and pepper. Sprinkle over plenty of
Parmesan cheese and serve immediately.

coriander chicken parcels with roasted vine tomatoes

preparation time **8 mins**
cooking time **19 mins**
total time **27 mins** serves **4**

4 bunches cherry tomatoes on the vine
2 tablespoons extra virgin olive oil
4 skinless chicken breast fillets
1 garlic clove, crushed
2 tablespoons chopped coriander
50 g/2 oz softened unsalted butter
pinch of ground cayenne pepper
8 slices Parma ham
salt and pepper

one Place the tomatoes, still attached to the vine, in a large roasting tin, drizzle over half the oil and season with salt and pepper. Set aside. Make a horizontal slit in the thickest side of each chicken breast.

two Beat the garlic and coriander into the butter with the cayenne pepper and some salt. Divide the flavoured butter into 4, pat flat and slip a piece into each chicken breast.

three Wrap 2 slices of Parma ham around each chicken breast and secure with cocktail sticks. Heat the remaining oil in a frying pan and brown the chicken parcels for 2 minutes on each side.

four Add the chicken to the tomatoes and roast in a preheated oven, 200°C (400°F), Gas Mark 6 for 10 minutes, until the chicken is cooked through. Remove the chicken, wrap it loosely in foil and leave to rest. Roast the tomatoes for a further 5 minutes.

five Remove the cocktail sticks from the chicken and serve it with the tomatoes and drizzled with the pan juices.

fillet steak with blue cheese and walnut sauce

preparation time **10 mins**
cooking time **4 mins**
total time **14 mins** serves **4**

25 g/1 oz butter
4 fillet steaks
new potatoes, to serve

BLUE CHEESE AND WALNUT SAUCE
1 garlic clove, crushed
25 g/1 oz parsley leaves, roughly chopped
15 g/½ oz mint leaves, roughly chopped
1 tablespoon roughly chopped walnuts
75 ml/3 fl oz extra virgin olive oil
2 tablespoons walnut oil
50 g/2 oz Roquefort cheese, crumbled
15 g/½ oz Parmesan cheese, grated
salt and pepper

one First, make the sauce. Put the garlic, parsley, mint, walnuts and both oils in a food processor and process until fairly smooth.
two Add the Roquefort and Parmesan and process again. Season with salt and pepper.
three Melt the butter in a heavy-based frying pan. Season the steaks with salt and pepper and fry for 2 minutes each side for rare, or a little longer for medium rare. Transfer to plates, top with the cheese sauce and serve with new potatoes.

The remaining sauce, topped
with a layer of oil, can be stored
in a screw-top jar for up to 5 days.

lamb fillet with beetroot and mint salad

preparation time **5 mins**
cooking time **20 mins**
total time **25 mins** serves **4**

125 g/4 oz Puy lentils
125 g/4 oz fine green beans
4 tablespoons extra virgin olive oil
2 lamb fillets (best end), about 300 g/10 oz each
4 tablespoons red wine
1 tablespoon red wine vinegar
375 g/12 oz cooked beetroot in natural juices, drained and diced
a small bunch mint, roughly chopped
salt and pepper

one Put the lentils into a saucepan, cover with cold water and simmer for 20 minutes. Drain well and transfer to a bowl.
two Meanwhile, blanch the green beans in lightly salted, boiling water for 3 minutes. Drain and pat dry on kitchen paper.
three Heat 1 tablespoon of the oil in a frying pan and fry the lamb fillets for 7 minutes for rare lamb. Transfer to a low oven, 150°C (300°F), Gas Mark 2, to rest for 5 minutes, reserving the juices in the pan.
four Add the wine to the pan juices and boil until only about 1 tablespoon remains. Remove from the heat and whisk in the vinegar and the remaining oil and season to taste with salt and pepper.
five Combine the lentils, beans, beetroot and mint leaves in a bowl, add the dressing and toss to coat. Serve with the lamb.

The cut of meat you need for this dish is the best end of
neck fillet or lamb loins. It is the eye fillet of the cutlets that
make up a rack, and it is quite an expensive cut. You can ask
to keep the ribs to cook as barbecued spare ribs.

poached apricots with rosewater and pistachios

preparation time **10 mins**
cooking time **5 mins**, plus cooling
total time **25 mins** serves **4**

125 g/4 oz caster sugar
300 ml/½ pint water
2 strips lemon rind
2 cardamom pods
1 vanilla pod
12 apricots, halved and pitted
1 tablespoon lemon juice
1 tablespoon rosewater
25 g/1 oz shelled pistachio nuts,
   finely chopped
vanilla ice cream or Greek yogurt,
   to serve (optional)

one Place a large bowl in the freezer to chill. Put the sugar and water into a wide saucepan and heat gently to dissolve the sugar. Meanwhile, cut the lemon rind into thin strips, crush the cardamom pods and split the vanilla pod in half. Add the lemon rind, cardamom and vanilla pod to the pan.

two Add the apricots and simmer gently for about 5 minutes, until softened. Remove from the heat, add the lemon juice and rosewater and transfer to the chilled bowl. Leave to cool until required.

three Spoon the apricots and a little of the syrup into serving bowls, scatter with the pistachio nuts and serve with vanilla ice cream or yogurt, if liked.

chocolate rum soufflés

preparation time **12 mins**
cooking time **15 mins**
total time **27 mins** serves **6**

125 g/4 oz dark chocolate
50 g/2 oz butter, plus extra for greasing
4 eggs, separated
75 g/3 oz caster sugar
2 tablespoons rum
clotted cream, to serve

one Melt the chocolate and butter in a small saucepan over a low heat. Meanwhile, beat together the egg yolks and sugar until creamy, then stir in the rum and melted chocolate mixture.

two Whisk the egg whites until stiff and fold into the chocolate mixture until evenly incorporated. Spoon into 6 greased ramekins and bake in a preheated oven, 200°C (400°F), Gas Mark 6, for 15 minutes, until risen. Serve immediately with clotted cream.

honeyed peaches with ginger cream

preparation time **5 mins**
cooking time **25 mins**
total time **30 mins** serves **4**

4 ripe peaches
2 tablespoons clear honey
seeds from 1 vanilla pod
juice of ½ lime
125 ml/4 fl oz double cream
1 tablespoon stem ginger syrup,
    from the jar
1 small piece stem ginger, diced

one Cut the peaches in half, remove the stones and arrange the halves, cut-side up, in an ovenproof dish.
two Combine the honey, vanilla seeds and lime juice and spoon over the peaches. Bake in a preheated oven, 220°C (425°F), Gas Mark 7, for 25 minutes.
three Whip the cream with the ginger syrup until it holds its shape. Fold the stem ginger into the whipped cream and serve with the baked peaches.

tiramisu trifles

preparation time **15 mins**
chilling time **15 mins**
total time **30 mins** serves **4**

8 amaretti biscuits
2 tablespoons Marsala
2 tablespoons cold espresso coffee
75 g/3 oz raspberries
50 g/2 oz dark chocolate, grated
125 g/4 oz mascarpone cheese
125 ml/4 fl oz crème fraîche
25 g/1 oz icing sugar
2 egg whites

one Lightly crumble the amaretti biscuits into 4 glasses. Combine the Marsala and coffee and pour half the mixture over the biscuits. Add the raspberries and sprinkle half the grated chocolate over the top.
two Beat the mascarpone, crème fraîche and the remaining Marsala mixture with the icing sugar until smooth. Whisk the egg whites until stiff, then fold into the Marsala cream and spoon into the glasses.
three Sprinkle the remaining chocolate over the trifles and chill until required.

storecupboard
suppers

Don't be concerned about the occasional last minute arrival; your storecupboard will most probably contain enough raw materials to put together a delicious impromptu feast. Pulses, grains and pastas are all staples that keep well and can be transformed into some of our favourite dishes. Remember, too, if one of the following recipes calls for an ingredient you don't have, then ad lib and substitute an equivalent that you do have.

broad bean hummus

preparation time **4 mins**
cooking time **4 mins**
total time **8 mins** serves **4** as a starter

250 g/8 oz broad beans
1 garlic clove, crushed
2 tablespoons chopped mint
1 tablespoon lemon juice
4 tablespoons extra virgin olive oil
25 g/1 oz Parmesan cheese, grated
salt and pepper

TO SERVE
vegetable crudités
bread sticks

one Cook the beans in a pan of lightly salted, boiling water for 3–4 minutes, until tender. Drain and refresh in cold water, then pat dry with kitchen paper.
two Place the beans, garlic, mint, lemon juice and oil in a food processor or blender and process to form a smooth paste.
three Transfer to a bowl, add the cheese and season to taste with salt and pepper. Serve with a selection of vegetable crudités and bread sticks for dipping.

This bean hummus is particularly versatile as it can be served as a dip with a selection of crudités, as a sandwich filling or a sauce for pasta.

artichoke and blue cheese panini

preparation time **7 mins**
cooking time **6 mins**
total time **13 mins** serves **2**

400 g/13 oz can artichoke hearts, drained
   and rinsed
125 g/4 oz Cambozola or Dolcelatte cheese
1 small ripe pear
2 focaccia rolls
a few watercress sprigs
salt and pepper

one Pat the artichokes dry and cut into thin slices. Thinly slice the cheese. Peel, core and thinly slice the pear.
two Halve the focaccia and toast the cut sides in a hot griddle pan or under a hot grill. Fill with the artichokes, cheese, pear slices and watercress. Season to taste with salt and pepper and sandwich together.
three Lower the heat and griddle the whole rolls for 2 minutes on each side, until toasted and the cheese starts to melt.

This is a good basic sauce for pasta and can be made without the bacon for vegetarians. I often make up several batches, minus the mascarpone or crème fraîche, and freeze it for future use.

tomato and bacon sauce for pasta

preparation time **3 mins**
cooking time **15 mins**
total time **18 mins** makes enough sauce
for **4** servings of pasta

2 garlic cloves, crushed
2 x 400 g/13 oz cans chopped tomatoes
4 tablespoons extra virgin olive oil
1 teaspoon dried oregano
1 teaspoon caster sugar
8 rashers smoked back bacon, finely chopped
75 g/3 oz mascarpone cheese or
    75 ml/3 fl oz crème fraîche
salt and pepper
pasta, to serve

one Put the garlic, tomatoes, oil, oregano and sugar into a saucepan. Season to taste with salt and pepper and bring to the boil; cover and simmer for 10 minutes.
two Add the bacon and simmer, uncovered, for a further 5 minutes.
three Stir in the mascarpone or crème fraîche, heat through then taste and adjust the seasoning if necessary. Serve with freshly cooked pasta.

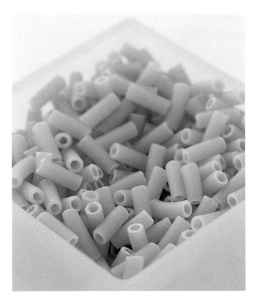

smoked tuna and bean salad

preparation time **10 mins**
cooking time **11 mins**
total time **21 mins** serves **4**

250 g/8 oz baby new potatoes
125 g/4 oz fine green beans
2 x 125 g/4 oz cans smoked tuna in olive
    oil, drained
400 g/13 oz can borlotti beans, drained
4 ripe plum tomatoes, roughly chopped
50 g/2 oz Niçoise olives
2 tablespoons capers in brine, drained
    and rinsed

DRESSING
2 sun-dried tomatoes in oil, drained and
    roughly chopped
1 small garlic clove, crushed
½ teaspoon dried oregano
1 tablespoon white wine vinegar
pinch of sugar
6 tablespoons extra virgin olive oil
salt and pepper

one Cook the potatoes in a pan of lightly
salted, boiling water for 8 minutes. Add
the green beans and cook for a further
3 minutes, until both the potatoes and
beans are tender. Drain and refresh in cold
water, drain again, then pat dry and place
in a large bowl.
two Meanwhile, flake the tuna. Add the
tuna, borlotti beans, tomatoes, olives and
capers to the potatoes.
three To make the dressing, put the sun-
dried tomatoes, garlic, oregano, vinegar,
sugar and oil in a food processor and work
to a purée. Season with salt and pepper.
Pour over the salad, toss well and serve.

chilli bean soup

preparation time **8 mins**
cooking time **22 mins**
total time **30 mins** serves **3–4**

2 tablespoons olive oil
1 onion, chopped
1 garlic clove, crushed
1 teaspoon hot chilli powder
1 teaspoon ground coriander
½ teaspoon ground cumin
400 g/13 oz can red kidney beans, drained
400 g/13 oz can chopped tomatoes
600 ml/1 pint vegetable stock
12 tortilla chips
50 g/2 oz Cheddar cheese, grated
salt and pepper
soured cream, to serve

one Heat the oil in a saucepan and fry the
onion, garlic, chilli powder, coriander and
cumin, stirring frequently, for 5 minutes,
until the onion has softened. Add the beans,
tomatoes and stock and season to taste
with salt and pepper.
two Bring the soup to the boil, cover and
simmer for 15 minutes. Transfer to a food
processor or blender and process until fairly
smooth. Pour into heatproof bowls.
three Place tortilla chips on top of the soup,
scatter over the grated cheese and grill for
1–2 minutes, until the cheese has melted.
Serve immediately with soured cream.

individual macaroni cheeses

preparation time **5 mins**
cooking time **20 mins**
total time **25 mins** serves **4**

spicy tuna fish cakes

preparation time **10 mins**
cooking time **18 mins**
total time **28 mins** serves **4**

250 g/8 oz floury potatoes, diced
2 x 200 g/7 oz cans tuna in olive oil, drained
50 g/2 oz Cheddar cheese, grated
4 spring onions, finely chopped
1 small garlic clove, crushed
2 teaspoons dried thyme
1 small egg, beaten
½ teaspoon cayenne pepper
4 tablespoons seasoned flour
salt and pepper
vegetable oil, for frying

TO SERVE
mixed green salad
mayonnaise

one Cook the potatoes in a pan of lightly salted, boiling water for 10 minutes, until tender. Drain well, mash and cool slightly.
two Meanwhile, flake the tuna. Beat the tuna, cheese, spring onions, garlic, thyme and egg into the mashed potato. Season to taste with cayenne, salt and pepper.
three Divide the mixture into 4 and shape into thick patties. Dust with seasoned flour and fry in a shallow layer of vegetable oil for 5 minutes on each side, until crisp and golden. Serve the fish cakes hot with a mixed green salad and mayonnaise.

250 g/8 oz macaroni
4 rashers smoked back bacon, diced
1 garlic clove, crushed
150 ml/¼ pint single cream
150 ml/¼ pint milk
pinch of freshly grated nutmeg
175 g/6 oz hard cheese, such as Cheddar
    or Gruyére, grated
4 tablespoons chopped basil
salt and pepper

one Cook the macaroni in a pan of lightly salted, boiling water for 10–12 minutes, until tender but still firm to the bite. Drain and place in a large bowl.
two Meanwhile, dry-fry the bacon in a small frying pan until browned but not crisp. Add the garlic, fry for 1 minute and then add the cream and milk and season with a little nutmeg. Bring just to boiling point.
three Stir in 125 g/4 oz of the cheese and all the basil, remove from the heat and stir until the cheese melts. Season to taste with salt and pepper and stir into the macaroni.
four Spoon into individual gratin dishes, top with the remaining cheese and bake in a preheated oven, 230°C (450°F), Gas Mark 8, for 10 minutes, until golden.

asian-style risotto

preparation time **7 mins**
cooking time **23 mins**
total time **30 mins** serves **4**

1.2 litres/2 pints hot vegetable stock
1 tablespoon dark soy sauce
2 tablespoons mirin
3 tablespoons sunflower oil
1 tablespoon sesame oil
1 bunch spring onions, thickly sliced
2 garlic cloves, chopped
2.5 cm/1 inch piece of fresh root ginger, peeled
 and grated
375 g/12 oz risotto rice
6 lime leaves
250 g/8 oz shiitake mushrooms
15 g/¹/₂ oz coriander, chopped
coriander sprigs, to garnish

one Put the stock, soy sauce and mirin into a
pan and bring to a very gentle simmer.
two Meanwhile, heat 2 tablespoons of the
sunflower oil and the sesame oil and fry the
spring onions, garlic and ginger over a high
heat for 1 minute. Add the rice and lime
leaves, stir until the grains are glossy, then
add 150 ml/¼ pint of the stock. Stir until the
liquid has been absorbed.
three Continue to add the stock, a little at a
time, stirring frequently, until almost all the
liquid is absorbed.
four Meanwhile, wipe the mushrooms,
discard the stalks and thinly slice all but a
few. Fry all the mushrooms in the remaining
oil for 5 minutes until golden.
five Add the coriander, mushrooms and the
remaining stock to the risotto. Heat through
and serve garnished with the reserved whole
mushrooms and coriander sprigs.

mustard rarebit with caraway

preparation time **3 mins**
cooking time **10 mins**
total time **13 mins** serves **4**

25 g/1 oz butter
4 spring onions, thinly sliced
½ teaspoon caraway seeds
250 g/8 oz Cheddar or Red Leicester
 cheese, grated
50 ml/2 fl oz strong ale
2 teaspoons wholegrain mustard
4 slices white bread
pepper

one Melt the butter in a small pan, add the
spring onions and caraway seeds and fry for
5 minutes, until the onions have softened.
two Stir in the cheese with the beer and
mustard, season with pepper to taste and
melt over a very low heat.
three Meanwhile, toast the bread lightly on
both sides and place on a foil-lined grill pan.
Pour over the cheese mixture and grill for
1 minute, until bubbling and golden.

mushroom and chickpea curry with aromatic rice

preparation time **5 mins**
cooking time **25 mins**
total time **30 mins** serves **4**

50 g/2 oz butter
1 onion, chopped
2 garlic cloves, crushed
2.5 cm/1 inch piece of fresh root ginger,
    peeled and grated
250 g/8 oz button mushrooms
2 tablespoons hot curry powder
1 teaspoon ground coriander
1 teaspoon ground cinnamon
375 g/12 oz potatoes, diced
400 g/13 oz can chickpeas, drained
50 g/2 oz cashew nuts
125 ml/4 fl oz Greek yogurt
2 unripe bananas, cut into chunks
chopped coriander (optional)
salt and pepper

AROMATIC RICE
375 g/12 oz long-grain rice
12 dried curry leaves
3 cardamom pods, crushed
1 cinnamon stick, crushed
1 teaspoon salt
750 ml/1½ pints water

one First cook the rice. Place the rice in a saucepan with the curry leaves, cardomom, cinnamon and salt. Add the water and bring to the boil then cover the pan and cook over a low heat for 10 minutes. Remove the pan from the heat, but leave the rice undisturbed for a further 10 minutes.

two Meanwhile, melt the butter in a frying pan and fry the onion, garlic, ginger and mushrooms for 5 minutes.

three Add the curry powder, ground coriander, cinnamon and potatoes, stir, and then add the chickpeas. Season to taste with salt and pepper and add just enough water to cover. Bring to the boil, cover and simmer gently for 15 minutes.

four While the curry is cooking, toast and roughly chop the cashew nuts. Stir them into the curry with the yogurt, bananas and chopped coriander, if using. Heat through without boiling and serve with the rice.

leek and goats' cheese frittata

preparation time **3 mins**
cooking time **17 mins**
total time **20 mins** serves **4**

25 g/1 oz butter
2 leeks, sliced
1 garlic clove, crushed
1 teaspoon chopped thyme
6 eggs
2 tablespoons chopped parsley
125 g/4 oz goats' cheese, sliced
25 g/1 oz pitted black olives, halved
salt and pepper

one Melt the butter in a frying pan and fry the leeks, garlic and thyme for 10 minutes, until the leeks have softened.
two Meanwhile, beat the eggs with the parsley and salt and pepper to taste.
three Swirl the egg mixture into the pan and cook for 3–4 minutes, until almost set through. Top with the goats' cheese and olives and cook under a hot grill for a further 2–3 minutes, until bubbling, golden and set.

sticky toffee puddings

preparation time **5 mins**
cooking time **20–25 mins**
total time **30 mins** serves **4**

4 tablespoons double cream, plus extra to serve
50 g/2 oz butter, separated into quarters
4 tablespoons soft light brown sugar

SPONGE
25 g/1 oz walnuts, finely chopped
125 g/4 oz softened butter
125 g/4 oz soft light brown sugar
2 eggs
75 g/3 oz self-raising flour

one Divide the cream, butter and sugar evenly between 4 ramekins or timbales.
two To make the sponge, put the walnuts, butter, sugar, eggs and flour in a food processor and process until smooth. Spoon the sponge mixture over the toffee mixture and smooth flat.
three Bake in a preheated oven, 190°C (375°F), Gas Mark 5, for 20–25 minutes, until risen and lightly golden. Turn out and serve with the extra cream, lightly whipped.

Surprisingly quick to prepare and cook, these nutty sticky puddings are really yummy!

Index

Acknowledgements

Executive Editor: Sarah Ford
Project Editor: Alice Tyler
Executive Art Editor: Geoff Fennell
Designer: Sue Michniewicz

Photographer: Ian Wallace
Stylist: Clare Hunt
Home Economist: Louise Pickford
Production Controller: Ian Paton